TEACHER'S PET PUBLICATIONS

LITPLAN TEACHER PACK
for
Where the Red Fern Grows
based on the book by
Wilson Rawls

Written by
Barbara M. Linde, MA Ed.

© 1996 Teacher's Pet Publications
All Rights Reserved

This **LitPlan** for Wilson Rawls's
Where The Red Fern Grows
has been brought to you by Teacher's Pet Publications, Inc.

Copyright Teacher's Pet Publications 1996
11504 Hammock Point
Berlin MD 21811

Only the student materials in this unit plan (such as worksheets, study questions, and tests) may be reproduced multiple times for use in the purchaser's classroom.

For any additional copyright questions,
contact Teacher's Pet Publications.

www.tpet.com

TABLE OF CONTENTS - *Where the Red Fern Grows*

Introduction	5
Unit Objectives	7
Unit Outline	8
Reading Assignment Sheet	9
Study Questions	13
Quiz/Study Questions (Multiple Choice)	25
Pre-Reading Vocabulary Worksheets	45
Lesson One (Introductory Lesson)	63
Nonfiction Assignment Sheet	67
Oral Reading Evaluation Form	69
Writing Assignment 1	71
Writing Evaluation Form	72
Writing Assignment 2	74
Writing Assignment 3	77
Extra Writing Assignments/Discussion ?s	80
Vocabulary Review Activities	85
Unit Review Activities	88
Unit Tests	95
Unit Resource Materials	133
Vocabulary Resource Materials	149

A FEW NOTES ABOUT THE AUTHOR
Wilson Rawls

RAWLS, Wilson (born 1913), U.S. author, born on September 24, 1913 in Scraper, Oklahoma. Rawls wrote books that appealed to young people, especially because of his fully developed animal characters.

Rawls had very little formal education, but his mother read stories to him as a child, He was especially influenced by Jack London's *Call of the Wild*. Rawls went to work as a carpenter, finding jobs in Mexico, South America, Alaska, and throughout the United States. He did not begin writing full-time until 1959. His novel *Summer of the Monkeys* (1976) received several awards, including the Sequoyah Children's Book Award, the Golden Archer Award, and the William Allen White Children's Book Award. He also wrote *Where the Red Fern Grows* (1961), which was a selection of the Literary Guild, and which was made into a motion picture.

Courtesy of Compton's Learning Company

INTRODUCTION

This unit has been designed to develop students' reading, writing, thinking, listening and speaking skills through exercises and activities related to *Where the Red Fern Grows* by Wilson Rawls. It includes nineteen lessons, supported by extra resource materials.

The **introductory lesson** introduces students to one main theme of the novel (the special kind of love that can exist between a person and their pet) through a bulletin board activity. Following the introductory activity, students are given an explanation of how the activity relates to the book they are about to read.

The **reading assignments** are approximately thirty pages each; some are a little shorter while others are a little longer. Students have approximately 15 minutes of pre-reading work to do prior to each reading assignment. This pre-reading work involves reviewing the study questions for the assignment and doing some vocabulary work for 8 to 10 vocabulary words they will encounter in their reading.

The **study guide questions** are fact-based questions; students can find the answers to these questions right in the text. These questions come in two formats: short answer or multiple choice. The best use of these materials is probably to use the short answer version of the questions as study guides for students (since answers will be more complete), and to use the multiple choice version for occasional quizzes. It might be a good idea to make transparencies of your answer keys for the overhead projector.

The **vocabulary work** is intended to enrich students' vocabularies as well as to aid in the students' understanding of the book. Prior to each reading assignment, students will complete a two-part worksheet for approximately 8 to 10 vocabulary words in the upcoming reading assignment. Part I focuses on students' use of general knowledge and contextual clues by giving the sentence in which the word appears in the text. Students are then to write down what they think the words mean based on the words' usage. Part II gives students dictionary definitions of the words and has them match the words to the correct definitions based on the words' contextual usage. Students should then have an understanding of the words when they meet them in the text.

After each reading assignment, students will go back and formulate answers for the study guide questions. Discussion of these questions serves as a **review** of the most important events and ideas presented in the reading assignments.

After students complete extra discussion questions, there is a **vocabulary review** lesson which pulls together all of the separate vocabulary lists for the reading assignments and gives students a review of all of the words they have studied.

Following the reading of the book, two lessons are devoted to the **extra discussion questions/writing assignments**. These questions focus on interpretation, critical analysis and personal response, employing a variety of thinking skills and adding to the students' understanding of the novel. These questions are done as a **group activity**. Using the information they have acquired so far through individual work and class discussions, students get together to further examine the text and to brainstorm ideas relating to the themes of the novel.

The group activity is followed by a **reports and discussion** session in which the groups share their ideas about the book with the entire class; thus, the entire class gets exposed to many different ideas regarding the themes and events of the book.

There are three **writing assignments** in this unit, each with the purpose of informing, persuading, or having students express personal opinions. The first assignment is to **inform**: students will compose a classified advertisement to sell something. The second assignment is to **persuade**: students will write a persuasive argument to convince their parents they should get a pet. The third assignment is to express a personal **opinion**: students will discuss the relative merits of living in an urban or a rural area.

In addition, there is a **nonfiction reading assignment**. Students are required to read a piece of nonfiction related in some way to *Where the Red Fern Grows*. After reading their nonfiction pieces, students will fill out a worksheet on which they answer questions regarding facts, interpretation, criticism, and personal opinions. During one class period, students make **oral presentations** about the nonfiction pieces they have read. This not only exposes all students to a wealth of information, it also gives students the opportunity to practice **public speaking**.

The **review lesson** pulls together all of the aspects of the unit. The teacher is given four or five choices of activities or games to use which all serve the same basic function of reviewing all of the information presented in the unit.

The **unit test** comes in two formats: all multiple choice-matching-true/false or with a mixture of matching, short answer, and composition. As a convenience, two different tests for each format have been included.

There are additional **support materials** included with this unit. The **resource sections** include suggestions for an in-class library, crossword and word search puzzles related to the novel, and extra vocabulary worksheets. There is a list of **bulletin board ideas** which gives the teacher suggestions for bulletin boards to go along with this unit. In addition, there is a list of **extra class activities** the teacher could choose from to enhance the unit or as a substitution for an exercise the teacher might feel is inappropriate for his/her class. **Answer keys** are located directly after the **reproducible student materials** throughout the unit. The student materials may be reproduced for use in the teacher's classroom without infringement of copyrights. No other portion of this unit may be reproduced without the written consent of Teacher's Pet Publications, Inc.

UNIT OBJECTIVES *Where the Red Fern Grows*

1. Through reading *Where the Red Fern Grows* students will analyze characters and their situations to better understand the themes of the novel.

2. Students will demonstrate their understanding of the text on four levels: factual, interpretive, critical, and personal.

3. Students will practice reading aloud and silently to improve their skills in each area.

4. Students will enrich their vocabularies and improve their understanding of the novel through the vocabulary lessons prepared for use in conjunction with it.

5. Students will answer questions to demonstrate their knowledge and understanding of the main events and characters in *Where the Red Fern Grows*

6. Students will practice writing through a variety of writing assignments.

7. The writing assignments in this are geared to several purposes:
   a. To check the students' reading comprehension;
   b. To make students think about the ideas presented by the novel;
   c. To make students put those ideas into perspective;
   d. To encourage critical and logical thinking;
   e. To provide the opportunity to practice good grammar and improve students' use of the English language.

8. Students will read aloud, report, and participate in large and small group discussions to improve their public speaking and personal interaction skills.

UNIT OUTLINE - *Where the Red Fern Grows*

1	2	3	4	5
Unit Intro Distribute Unit Materials PV I-IV	Read I-IV Study ?? I-IV	PVR V-VII Oral Reading Evaluation	Quiz I-VII PVR VIII-X	Writing Assignment #1
6	7	8	9	10
Study ?? VIII-X PVR XI-XII	Study ?? XI-XII PVR XIII-XIV	Study ?? XIII-XIV Writing Assignment #2	Writing Conference	Quiz VIII-XIV PVR XV-XVI
11	12	13	14	15
Writing Assignment #3	Study ?? XV-XVI PVR XVII-XVIII	Study ?? XVII-XVIII PV XIX-XX	R XIX-XX Study ?? XIX-XX	Extra Discussion ??
16	17	18	19	20
Library Work	Vocabulary Review	Group Work	Non-Fiction Assignment	Movie and Discussion
21	22			
Review	Test			

Key: P = Preview Study Questions   V = Vocabulary Work   R = Read

READING ASSIGNMENT SHEET *Where the Red Fern Grows*

Date to be Assigned	Chapters	Completion Date (Prior to Class on This Date)
	Chapters I-IV	
	Chapters V-VII	
	Chapters VIII-X	
	Chapters XI-XII	
	Chapters XIII-XIV	
	Chapters XV-XVI	
	Chapters XVII-XVIII	
	Chapters XIX-XV	

STUDY GUIDE QUESTIONS

SHORT ANSWER STUDY GUIDE QUESTIONS *Where the Red Fern Grows*

Chapters I, II, III, IV
1. By what method is the story told?
2. What is the setting of the novel?
3. Who is the main character of the story? Who are the other characters introduced in this section of the novel?
4. What "terrible disease" did the main character say he had?
5. What did Papa give the boy in place of what he wanted, and what was the result?
6. Why couldn't the boy have what he wanted?
7. Describe the boy's plan to get what he wanted.
8. How long did it take the boy to earn the money?
9. What was his grandfather's reaction when the boy told him of his plan?
10. Describe the boy's journey to pick up his purchase.

Chapters V, VI, VII
1. What is the boy's name?
2. Describe the events at the depot.
3. Describe what happened as Billy was walking through town.
4. What did Billy encounter while camping that night, and what did he do about it?
5. What did Billy name his dogs, and why did he give them those particular names?
6. Describe what happened when Billy arrived home with his dogs.
7. What did Billy's parents tell him they wanted to do someday, and why?
8. What was the next item that Billy needed, and why did he need it?
9. Whom did Billy talk to when he needed advice about hunting coons?
10. What did Billy say about his communication with his dogs?

Chapters VIII, IX
1. How did Billy's parents feel about his hunting?
2. How old was Billy when he went coon hunting for the first time?
3. What did Billy realize about the way his father was talking to him?
4. What feeling did Billy get on his first night of hunting, when Old Dan bawled the first time? What did he do after he also heard Little Ann's bawl?
5. Where had the hounds treed their first coon?
6. Describe Billy's thoughts and feelings when he saw where the hounds had treed their first coon.
7. How did the members of Billy's family feel about his decision?
8. How did Billy's grandfather keep the coon in the tree while Billy went home to rest?
9. What interesting news about coonskins did Billy's grandfather share with him?
10. What was the outcome of Billy's efforts?

Short Answer Study Guide Questions *Where the Red Fern Grows*

Chapters X, XI, XII
1. What happened to the first coon hide?
2. What did Billy do with the coon skins? What did he do with the money he made?
3. Describe both of Old Dan's predicaments and how they were resolved.
4. Describe Little Ann's predicament and how it was resolved.
5. What did Billy tell his parents about his evening's adventure?
6. What happened to Billy after he returned home?
7. Billy asked his mother if God answered all prayers. What was her reply?
8. What was the bet Billy's grandfather made with the Pritchard boys? Why did he make it?
9. Why did the Pritchard boys refer to the coon as "the ghost coon"?
10. At one point while the boys were watching the dogs chase the coon, Billy said he felt good all over. What did he feel good about?

Chapters XIII, XIV
1. Why did Billy pay off on his bet?
2. What caused Little Ann to throw up her head and whine?
3. Where was the coon?
4. What did Billy decide about the ghost coon, and why?
5. What did Rubin do when Billy asked for his money back?
6. What were the dogs doing while the boys were fighting?
7. What did Rubin do, and what was the result of his acions?
8. What did Billy do to show his sorrow for the incident?
9. What news did Billy's grandfather tell him a few days after the accident?
10. Who went on the trip?

Chapters XV-XVI
1. What happened on the trip that made Billy feel more grown up?
2. Which contest did Billy enter first, and what was the result?
3. Where did Billy think they should go on their first night of hunting?
4. Where did the hounds run the first coon, and what was the result?
5. How many coons did the dogs kill on their first night of competition?
6. What about the dogs surprised the judge?
7. Why did one of the hunters come around with a small box in his hands?
8. Where did Billy want to go hunting on the final night, and why?
9. The judge saw the two hounds stop and stare at Billy at the beginning of the hunt. What was Billy's explanation for their actions?
10. After the dogs killed the coon, what did they do that surprised the judge?

Short Answer Study Guide Questions *Where the Red Fern Grows*

Chapters XVII-XVIII
1. What was the weather like on this part of the hunt?
2. What did the judge think they should do, and what was Billy's reply? What did the men finally do?
3. Describe what happened to Billy's grandfather, including how he was found.
4. What did they do after they had made Grandpa comfortable?
5. Where did the dogs go?
6. What did the rest of the hunters do when they found Billy and the hunting party?
7. Describe what happened when they found the dogs.
8. What happened when they got back to camp?
9. Describe the events when Billy and his father arrived home.
10. What did Billy see his mother doing as he was preparing for bed?

Chapters XIX-XX
1. What animal did Billy think the dogs had treed the night they went to the Cyclone Timber country?
2. How did Billy feel about the animal the dogs had treed?
3. What unusual actions did Old Dan take, and how did Billy feel about it?
4. What animal had the dogs actually treed?
5. Describe the fight between the hounds and the other animal.
6. How did Billy feel about what his dogs had done?
7. What did Billy discover about Old Dan as they were walking home? What did he do about it?
8. What happened to the dogs?
9. What did Billy's parents tell him at dinner?
10. What did Billy discover the day the family left the Ozarks? What was the significance of the discovery?

ANSWER KEY: SHORT ANSWER STUDY GUIDE QUESTIONS
Where the Red Fern Grows

Chapters I-IV

1. By what method is the story told?
    It is introduced in the present time in Chapter I. From Chapter II on the story is told as a flashback.

2. What is the setting of the novel?
    The novel is set in a valley in the Ozark mountains in northeastern Oklahoma. The land the boy's family lived on was a strip that extended from the foothills of the Ozarks to the Illinois River.

3. Who is the main character of the story? Who are the other characters introduced in this section of the novel?
    The main character is a young boy. The reader does not discover his name until Chapter 5. The other characters are his mother, father, sisters, and grandfather.

4. What "terrible disease" did the main character say he had?
    He had puppy love; he wanted a dog.

5. What did Papa give the boy in place of what he wanted, and what was the result?
    Papa gave him three small steel traps. The cat kept getting caught until he finally left home. When the newness of the traps wore off, the boy went back to wanting a dog.

6. Why couldn't the boy have what he wanted?
    His parents were too poor and they couldn't afford it.

7. Describe the boy's plan to get what he wanted.
    He discovered an ad in an old piece of paper. The ad was from a kennel in Kentucky that was selling hound pups for twenty-five dollars each. He decided to earn the money to buy two hounds. The next morning he found a K.C. Baking Powder can and began using it for a bank. He caught crawfish and other small fish and sold them to the fishermen for bait. He also sold them fresh vegetables and roasting corn. He picked blackberries and sold them to his grandfather. He used his traps in the winter and sold the furs to his grandfather.

8. How long did it take the boy to earn the money?
    It took him two years.

9. What was his grandfather's reaction when the boy told him of his plan?
    The grandfather said he would help the boy, because he had worked so hard for what he wanted.

10. Describe the boy's journey to pick up his purchase.
    He walked to Talequah, a town about thirty miles from his home. He had never been to a town before, and he was rather scared. He saw his full reflection in a plate glass for the first time. He encountered some of the town children who made fun of him and called him a hillbilly. He went into the general store and bought overalls for his father, cloth for his mother, and candy for his sisters.

Chapters V-VII

1. What is the boy's name?
    His name is Billy Colman.

2. Describe the events at the depot.
    Billy was scared to go in. He walked around the depot first, then finally went in. The station master was friendly. He took Billy to the puppies. Billy began crying when he first held the puppies. The station master cut two holes in the gunny sack so the puppies could look out. Billy left with the puppies.

3. Describe what happened as Billy was walking through town.
    Several people stared at him, shouted questions, and laughed. Then some of the children ganged around him. One boy stomped on Billy's bare foot with his shoe, then pulled the girl puppy's ear. Billy began fighting with him and several other boys jumped in. They were beating and kicking Billy when the town marshal stopped them. The marshal chased the children away, made sure Billy was all right, and gave him his first taste of soda pop.

4. What did Billy encounter while camping that night, and what did he do about it?
    He and the dogs were sleeping in a cave. They heard the scream of a mountain lion. He built up the fire to keep it away. The boy dog went to the mouth of the cave and bawled at it.

5. What did Billy name his dogs, and why did he give them those particular names?
    He saw the names "Dan" and "Ann" carved in a tree. He called them "Old Dan" and "Little Ann."

6. Describe what happened when Billy arrived home with his dogs.
> His grandfather had told his parents what he had done. His father laughed, and his mother cried. They asked why Billy didn't tell them what he was doing. His sisters were thrilled with the puppies and began playing with them. His father opened the packages. Billy realized all was forgiven and his family liked the gifts.

7. What did Billy's parents tell him they wanted to do someday, and why?
> They said they wanted to move to town to give their children a better education and enable them to meet people.

8. What was the next item that Billy needed, and why did he need it?
> He needed a coonskin to train his dogs.

9. Whom did Billy talk to when he needed advice about hunting coons?
> He talked to his grandfather.

10. What did Billy say about his communication with his dogs?
> He said they could have heart-to-heart talks together. His dogs had a language of their own that was easy for him to understand. He could see answers in their eyes, in the way they wagged their tails, in their whines, and in the caress of their tongues.

Chapters VIII-IX

1. How did Billy's parents feel about his hunting?
> His mother was worried but felt she could not stop him because of all he had done to get the dogs. His father thought it was fine because he was getting to be a man.

2. How old was Billy when he went coon hunting for the first time?
> He was almost fourteen.

3. What did Billy realize about the way his father was talking to him?
> He realized his father was talking to him like he was a man.

4. What feeling did Billy get on his first night of hunting, when Old Dan bawled the first time? What did he do after he also heard Little Ann's bawl?
> He felt like a knot had been tied in his throat. Then he cried and whooped as the tears ran down his face.

5. Where had the hounds treed their first coon?
> The hounds had treed the coon in the largest sycamore on the bottoms. Billy had named it "the big tree."

6. Describe Billy's thoughts and feelings when he saw where the hounds had treed their first coon.
   At first, Billy felt discouraged because the tree was so big. He decided to let the coon go. He thought the dogs appeared to be disappointed, and then vowed to cut the tree down no matter what it took.

7. How did the members of Billy's family feel about his decision?
   His father and grandfather supported him wholeheartedly. At first his mother wanted him to stop. After she saw that Old Dan had stayed on the bottoms near the tree all night, she agreed that Billy should get the coon for the dogs. One of his sisters thought he was crazy.

8. How did Billy's grandfather keep the coon in the tree while Billy went home to rest?
   He made a scarecrow on the ground where the coon could see it.

9. What interesting news about coonskins did Billy's grandfather share with him?
   He said there was a fad in New England, and coonskin coats were in demand. He said it was driving the price of coonskins up, and Billy was in a position to make some money.

10. What was the outcome of Billy's efforts?
    Billy chopped until he had blisters on his hands and could not chop anymore. He was giving up when he asked God to help him. Shortly after, he heard the wind pick up in the top of the sycamore. The wind blew the tree over. Billy was sure the tree fell over because God was answering his prayer.

Chapters X, XI, XII
1. What happened to the first coon hide?
   Mama made a coonskin cap for Billy. He wore it proudly.

2. What did Billy do with the coon skins? What did he do with the money he made?
   He took the coon skins to his grandfather's store. His grandfather bought them. He gave the money to his father.

3. Describe both of Old Dan's predicaments and how they were resolved.
   Old Dan had followed a coon into an old muskrat den and was stuck. Billy dug him out and washed him off. Old Dan turned around and went back in after the coon. Billy and Little Ann helped dig the coon out and Old Dan killed him.
   Another time Old Dan climbed up inside a hollow tree and out onto a branch to get a baby coon. Billy climbed up after him and pushed him back down the hole. Then he climbed down the tree. He caught Old Dan's tail as he was climbing back up the tree, and pulled him out. Then he blocked up the hole with rocks.

4. Describe Little Ann's predicament and how it was resolved.
   Little Ann chased a coon out onto the ice covered river and she fell through the ice into the river. Billy said a prayer to ask God to save her. Then he took the handle off his lantern, bent a hook onto one end, and tied it to the end of a cane pole. He took off his clothes and waded out into the icy river, breaking the ice with his axe as he went. He used the pole to get the hook under Little Ann's collar and dragged her out of the water. Once back on the bank, he made a fire and rubbed her to thaw her out. He attributed the rescue to God's help.

5. What did Billy tell his parents about his evening's adventure?
   He didn't tell them anything.

6. What happened to Billy after he returned home?
   He got a cold and stayed home for three days.

7. Billy asked his mother if God answered all prayers. What was her reply?
   She said He only answered the ones that were from the heart. The person praying had to be sincere and believe in God.

8. What was the bet Billy's grandfather made with the Pritchard boys? Why did he make it?
   Rubin wanted Billy to bet two dollars that his hounds could tree a certain old coon. When Billy refused, Rubin and Raine started taunting him. Billy's grandfather got angry and agreed to the bet. He put up the two dollars.

9. Why did the Pritchard boys refer to the coon as "the ghost coon?"
   The coon was old and had been treed many times, but never caught. He always managed to escape, and the boys had not been able to figure out where he went.

10. At one point while the boys were watching the dogs chase the coon, Billy said he felt good all over. What did he feel good about?
    He was happy because Rainie was whooping and screaming. Billy thought it was the first time in Rainie's life that he had been so excited.

Chapters XIII, XIV

1. Why did Billy pay off on his bet?
   He had climbed the big oak tree twice and couldn't find the coon. His dogs had given up.

2. What caused Little Ann to throw up her head and whine?
   She caught the coon's scent when a breeze began stirring.

3. Where was the coon?
   It was hiding in a hollow gatepost.

4. What did Billy decide about the ghost coon, and why?
   He decided he didn't want to kill the old coon because it had lived there such a long time.

5. What did Rubin do when Billy asked for his money back?
   He refused to give the money back. He threatened to knife Billy if he told his grandfather what had happened. Then he knocked Billy down and started whipping him in the face with his hat.

6. What were the dogs doing while the boys were fighting?
   The Pritchard boys' dog, Old Blue, had provoked a fight with Old Dan. Little Ann joined in and the two of them were killing Old Blue.

7. What did Rubin do, and what was the result of his acions?
   He grabbed Billy's axe and ran towards the dogs, intending to kill Old Dan and Little Ann. He tripped on a small stick and fell on the axe blade. Rainie saw him and ran away, screaming. Billy went to him and Rubin asked him to remove the axe. Billy did so, and Rubin died. Then Billy ran home and told his father what had happened.

8. What did Billy do to show his sorrow for the incident?
   He took some flowers his sisters had given him and put them on Rubin's grave.

9. What news did Billy's grandfather tell him a few days after the accident?
   He told Billy there was to be a championship coon hunt. He had entered Old Dan and Little Ann in the competition, and they had been accepted.

10. Who went on the trip?
    Grandpa, Papa, Billy, and the dogs went.

Chapters XV, XVI
1. What happened on the trip that made Billy feel more grown up?
   His grandfather gave him a cup of coffee after dinner. He had never been allowed to drink coffee before.

2. Which contest did Billy enter first, and what was the result?
   He entered Little Ann in the beauty contest. She won first place and a small silver cup.

3. Where did Billy think they should go on their first night of hunting?
   He thought they should go far down river out of range of where the others had gone.

4. Where did the hounds run the first coon, and what was the result?
   They ran the coon near the camp. The men doused all of the fires and the coon ran straight through the camp.

5. How many coons did the dogs kill on their first night of competition?
   They killed three coons.

6. What about the dogs surprised the judge?
   He was surprised that the dogs were able to find the scent when the coon had gone so far out on the river bottoms.

7. Why did one of the hunters come around with a small box in his hands?
   He was collecting money for a jackpot for the winner.

8. Where did Billy want to go hunting on the final night, and why?
   He wanted to go back to the swamp because he thought more coons lived there. It would be easy for the hounds to tree the coons there because the area was the same distance from the mountains and the river.

9. The judge saw the two hounds stop and stare at Billy at the beginning of the hunt. What was Billy's explanation for their actions?
   He said he could feel that they knew the hunt was important.

10. After the dogs killed the coon, what did they do that surprised the judge?
    The dogs licked and doctored each other's wounds.

Chapters XVII-XVIII

1. What was the weather like on this part of the hunt?
   There was a sleet storm. It was cold and icy.

2. What did the judge think they should do, and what was Billy's reply? What did the men finally do?
   The judge said he thought they should all go back to camp, and leave the dogs where they were. Billy refused to leave his dogs. He said they would die before they would leave a coon in a tree. The three men finally agreed to stay with Billy and look for the dogs.

3. Describe what happened to Billy's grandfather, including how he was found.
>He caught his foot in the fork of a broken elder limb. He was unconscious from the pain. Little Ann found him and Papa and the judge revived him. They carried him to a nearby gully and made him as comfortable as possible.

4. What did they do after they had made Grandpa comfortable?
>They returned their attention to the dogs and the coon hunt. The dogs killed another coon.

5. Where did the dogs go?
>They went off in the direction to which Billy had pointed to find one of the coons who had previously escaped.

6. What did the rest of the hunters do when they found Billy and the hunting party?
>Half of them took Grandpa back to camp to the doctor. The others went with Billy, his father, and the judge to find the dogs.

7. Describe what happened when they found the dogs.
>The dogs were covered with ice and were walking in a circle around the treed coon. The men built a fire to thaw the dogs out. The dogs killed the coon, giving Billy his third skin of the night.

8. What happened when they got back to camp?
>The other hunters awarded Billy the cup and the money.

9. Describe the events when Billy and his father arrived home.
>The girls ran to the wagon. Billy gave the two older girsl the small silver cup. He gave the large gold cup to the youngest girl. Then he gave the box of money to his mother. She looked at it and said her prayers had been answered.

10. What did Billy see his mother doing as he was preparing for bed?
>He saw his mother take two plates of food out to the doghouse. She knelt in prayer in front of them. When they had finished their food, she started petting them.

Chapters XIX-XX

1. What animal did Billy think the dogs had treed the night they went to the Cyclone Timber country?
>He thought they had treed a bobcat.

2. How did Billy feel about the animal the dogs had treed?
   He didn't like to have his dogs tree them because their fur was no good and the hounds usually got cut up.

3. What unusual actions did Old Dan take, and how did Billy feel about it?
   He curled back his lips, snarled, and then growled. Billy was scared and called to him, but he would not leave.

4. What animal had the dogs actually treed?
   It was a mountain lion.

5. Describe the fight between the hounds and the other animal.
   Old Dan met the mountain lion in mid air. Little Ann joined the fight. Billy joined in, fighting with his axe. When the lion charged at Billy, his dogs got between him and the lion. Billy returned to the fight and finally sank the blade into the lion's back. The lion died.

6. How did Billy feel about what his dogs had done?
   He was proud and grateful.

7. What did Billy discover about Old Dan as they were walking home? What did he do about it?
   Old Dan's belly had been slashed and his entrails were falling out. Billy pushed the entrails back into the wound and carried Old Dan home.

8. What happened to the dogs?
   Old Dan died soon after they arrived home. Billy buried him. A few days later Little Ann went to Old Dan's grave and died. The next day Billy buried her next to Old Dan.

9. What did Billy's parents tell him at dinner?
   They had saved all of the money he had made and they had enough to move the family to town. They said their prayers had been answered because of the dogs.

10. What did Billy discover the day the family left the Ozarks? What was the significance of the discovery?
    He found a red fern growing between the two dogs' graves. According to an old Indian legend, any spot where the red fern grew was sacred.

MULTIPLE CHOICE STUDY GUIDE/QUIZ QUESTIONS *Where the Red Fern Grows*

Chapters I, II, III, IV

1. True or False: The story is introduced in the present time in Chapter I. From Chapter II on the story is told as a first person flashback.
    A. True
    B. False

2. What is the setting of the novel?
    A. It is set in the Sycamore Swamp in southern Tennessee.
    B. It is set in the Ozark mountains in northeastern Oklahoma.
    C. It is set on the Talequah River Bottoms in southwestern Illinois.
    D. It is set on a Cherokee reservation in Kentucky.

3. Which of the following characters is *not* in the novel?
    A. Sister Ann
    B. a young boy
    C. Mama
    D. Grandpa

4. The main character defined puppy love as the first time he was in love with a girl.
    A. True
    B. False

5. What did Papa give the boy in place of what he wanted?
    A. He gave the boy a shotgun.
    B. He gave the boy his own horse and saddle.
    C. He gave the boy a thoroughbred collie pup.
    D. Papa gave him three small steel traps.

6. Why couldn't the boy have what he wanted?
    A. His parents were too poor and they couldn't afford it.
    B. It was against his parents' religious beliefs.
    C. His parents didn't want to spoil him by giving him everything he asked for.
    D. His mother thought he was too young to have the object he wanted.

7. How did the boy earn the money to get what he wanted?
    A. He worked in other men's fields. He grew vegetables and sold them to tourists. He picked blackberries and sold them to his grandfather. He trapped small animals and sold the furs to his grandfather.
    B. He sold bait, fresh vegetables, and roasting corn to the fishermen. He picked blackberries and sold them to his grandfather. His grandfather paid him to deliver items from the store to the customers.
    C. He cleaned and skinned fish for the fishermen, planted and maintained gardens for the neighboring women, and did odd jobs around his grandfather's store.
    D. He sold bait, fresh vegetables, and roasting corn to the fishermen. He picked blackberries and sold them to his grandfather. He trapped small animals and sold the furs to his grandfather.

8. How long did it take the boy to earn the money?
    A. It took him six months.
    B. It took him two years.
    C. It took him three months.
    D. It took him four years.

9. What was his grandfather's reaction when the boy told him of his plan?
    A. His grandfather thought it was a bad idea and he would not help.
    B. His grandfather said since he had done such a good job getting the money he could do the rest of the work himself as well.
    C. His grandfather said he would help the boy, because he had worked so hard for what he wanted.
    D. His grandfather said he had to ask his parents' permission to make the purchase.

10. Which did **not** happen on the boy's journey to pick up his purchase?
    A. He stole cloth, candy, and overalls from the general store.
    B. He walked to a town about thirty miles from his home.
    C. He had never been to a town before, and he was rather scared.
    D. He saw his full reflection in a plate glass for the first time.

Multiple Choice Study Guide/Quiz Questions *Where the Red Fern Grows*
Chapters V, VI, VII

1. The boy's first name was Billy. What was his last name?
    A. His last name was Colby.
    B. His last name was Cole.
    C. His last name was Collins.
    D. His last name was Colman.

2. What did Billy do when he first held his puppies?
    A. He began crying when he first held the puppies.
    B. He brushed their coats with his own hairbrush.
    C. He checked to make sure they were not deformed.
    D. He kissed each of them on the nose.

3. What did the town children do when they saw Billy walking along with his puppies?
    A. They admired the puppies and asked to pet them.
    B. They made fun of him and then began beating and kicking him.
    C. They called for the marshal to run Billy out of town.
    D. They ignored him completely, saying hillbillies were not worth noticing.

4. Which of the following happened while Billy and the puppies were camping on their return from town?
    A. There was a rattlesnake in their cave. The girl dog pounced on it and killed it.
    B. A group of boys from town followed them and harassed them. They took refuge in a cave. The boys were starting to roll a stone across the entrance when the marshal came and took them all back to town.
    C. They heard the scream of a mountain lion. Billy built up the fire to keep it away. The boy dog went to the mouth of the cave and bawled at it.
    D. They came across a cave where an old Cherokee Indian lived. He invited them in, fed them, and told them stories until they fell asleep.

5. True or False: Billy saw the names "Dan" and "Ann" carved in a tree. Then he named the puppies "Old Dan" and "Little Ann."
    A. True
    B. False

6. True or False: Billy's parents were furious when he got home. They said he had to send the dogs back and give them the money.
   A. True
   B. False

7. What did Billy's parents tell him they wanted to do someday, and why?
   A. They said they wanted him to take over the farm in about ten years. They said it was time for him to start learning the business from his father.
   B. They said they wanted to own more land. They wanted him to keep doing odd jobs and also start to hunt for furs so he could contribute his money to their plan.
   C. They said they wanted him to be a doctor. They planned to send him to boarding school in Oklahoma City and then to the medical school there.
   D. They said they wanted to move to town to give their children a better education and enable them to meet people.

8. What was the next item that Billy needed, and why did he need it?
   A. He needed leather to make collars for the dogs.
   B. He needed a coonskin to train his dogs.
   C. He needed a rifle to kill the coons when he took the dogs hunting.
   D. He needed a hunting license so he could hunt legally.

9. What did Billy do when he needed advice about hunting coons?
   A. He talked to his father.
   B. He talked to a neighbor.
   C. He talked to his grandfather.
   D. He wrote to the kennel in Kentucky where he had bought the dogs.

10. What did Billy say about his communication with his dogs?
    A. He said they could have heart-to-heart talks together. His dogs had a language of their own that was easy for him to understand.
    B. He said they were dumb animals who needed to be trained to take orders.
    C. He said Little Ann was able to communicate, but Old Dan wasn't because he was deaf.
    D. He said Little Ann would only communicate with his sisters, and Old Dan would only communicate with him.

Multiple Choice Study Guide/Quiz Questions *Where the Red Fern Grows*
Chapters VIII-IX

1. How did Billy's parents feel about his hunting?
   A. They both approved wholeheartedly. They said it was the way of the mountain folk and they were proud of him for carrying on the tradition.
   B. His mother strongly disapproved and wanted him to stop. His father told his mother that he was the head of the family and would make the decision. He said it was fine.
   C. His parents both disapproved but his grandfather convinced them to let him try it. He said Billy would get bored after a week or so and stop hunting.
   D. His mother was worried but felt she could not stop him because of all he had done to get the dogs. His father thought it was fine because he was getting to be a man.

2. How old was Billy when he went coon hunting for the first time?
   A. He was ten.
   B. He was thirteen.
   C. He was sixteen.
   D. He was twelve.

3. True or False: Billy realized his father was talking to him like he was a man.
   A. True
   B. False

4. What feeling did Billy get on his first night of hunting, when Old Dan bawled the first time? What did he do after he also heard Little Ann's bawl?
   A. He felt like a knot had been tied in his throat. Then he cried and whooped as the tears ran down his face.
   B. He was terrified to be out in the woods alone at night. He realized he had made a big mistake.
   C. He didn't realize what the sounds meant. He hit the dogs and told them to be quiet and not scare away the coons.
   D. He felt like he had finally become a man, and no one could tell him what to do.

5. Where did the hounds tree their first coon?
   A. They treed it in the largest sycamore on the bottoms.
   B. The treed it in his mother's favorite shade tree near the house.
   C. They treed it in an oak tree across the river where he couln't go to get it.
   D. They treed it on another farmer's property and he would not let them on to get it.

6. What did Billy decide to do about the treed coon?
    A. He was satisfied that they treed the coon. He said he didn't need to kill it to prove they were competent hunters.
    B. He said he would help his dogs get the coon out of the tree no matter what it took.
    C. He set traps around the bottom of the tree so the coon would get caught if it tried to climb down.
    D. He decided to let his father and grandfather catch the coon since they had more experience than he did.

7. What did the members of Billy's family think about his decision?
    A. His parents did not like his decision but his grandfather did.
    B. None of the family members thought he was making a wise choice.
    C. His father thought he was old enough to make his own decision. His mother and grandfather thought he should do what they wanted.
    D. His father and grandfather supported him. His mother finally agreed with him.

8. How did Billy's grandfather keep the coon in the tree while Billy went home to rest?
    A. He stayed at the bottom of the tree and fired his shotgun in the air every fifteen minutes.
    B. He built a fire at the base of the tree.
    C. He made a scarecrow on the ground where the coon could see it.
    D. He had the little girls march around the tree and bang on pots and pans.

9. Billy's grandfather said something was driving the price of coon skins up. What was it?
    A. People were watching the Daniel Boone series on television and wanted to own coon skin caps like Daniel Boone's.
    B. The government was getting ready to regulate the number of coons that could be killed, so people were buying as much as they could before the regulations went into effect.
    C. There was coon skin coat fad in New England, and coon skins were in high demand.
    D. The coons in a few neighboring states had a disease that made their skins unusable. The skins from Oklahoma were in the best around at the time.

10. What was the outcome of Billy's efforts?
    A. He gave up and left the tree alone.
    B. He asked his father and grandfather to help him and they all chopped the tree down.
    C. He succeeded in chopping through the entire tree in five days.
    D. He chopped through most of the tree, and then the wind blew it over.

Multiple Choice Study Guide/Quiz Questions *Where the Red Fern Grows*
Chapters X, XI, XII

1. What happened to the first coon hide?
    A. Mama made a coonskin cap for Billy.
    B. Billy gave it to his mother to make a fur collar for her coat.
    C. Billy gave it to his sisters to use as a doll blanket.
    D. Grandpa took it and hung it up in the store.

2. What did Billy do with the money he made from selling the coon skins?
    A. He kept it in his K. C. Baking Powder can.
    B. He gave it to his grandfather to put in his bank account.
    C. He gave the money to his father.
    D. He bought clothes and other things for the family, including a mule for his father.

3. What were Old Dan's predicaments, and how were they resolved?
    A. Old Dan climbed a tree and couldn't get down. Billy climbed a ladder to bring him down. He also got his paw stuck in a steel trap and Billy pried it loose.
    B. Old Dan got too close to a skunk and was sprayed. Billy gave him a bath every day for two weeks to get the smell out. He also got stuck in a beaver den, and Billy and Little Ann dug him out.
    C. Old Dan fell into a patch of poison ivy. Billy petted him and they both had poison ivy for several weeks. He also tried to jump a barbed wire fence and got cut up.
    D. Old Dan got stuck in an old muskrat den, and Billy and Little Ann dug him out. He also climbed up inside a hollow tree and out onto a branch. Billy climbed up after him and pushed him back down the hole.

4. How did Billy rescue Little Ann when she fell through the ice into the river?
    A. He put a piece of meat on a long pole and stretched it out to Little Ann. When she bit on the meat he pulled on the pole and dragged her in.
    B. He made a hook from his lantern handle and tied it to a pole. He waded out into the river, got the hook under her collar, and dragged her out of the water.
    C. The water was only waist deep on him. He waded out, breaking the ice with his axe. He put Little Ann under one arm and waded back to shore with her.
    D. He tied a rope around his waist and around a tree. He walked out as far as he could. Then he used another rope to lasso Little Ann and pull her out.

5. True or False: Billy told his parents all about his evening's adventure?
    A. True
    B. False

6. What happened to Billy after he returned home?
   A. He got pneumonia and stayed in bed for two weeks.
   B. He found out he had a broken arm and needed a cast.
   C. He got a cold and stayed home for three days.
   D. He had severe frostbite and lost two toes.

7. Billy asked his mother if God answered all prayers. What was her reply?
   A. She said He only answered the ones that were from the heart.
   B. She said He only answered prayers if the person praying helped himself first.
   C. She said He answered everyone's prayers all of the time.
   D. She said He didn't answer prayers, He did what He thought was best for the person.

8. What was the bet Billy's grandfather made with the Pritchard boys?
   A. He bet five dollars that Billy and his hounds could kill more coons in one night than they could with their hound.
   B. He bet two dollars that Billy's hounds could tree a certain old coon.
   C. He bet three dollars that Old Dan and Little Ann could follow a trail longer than the Pritchard boys' dogs could.
   D. He bet four dollars that Billy's hounds could tree a coon faster than the Pritchard boys' hounds could.

9. True or False: The Pritchard boys refer to the coon as "the ghost coon" because it was all white.
   A. True
   B. False

10. At one point while the boys were watching the dogs chase the coon, Billy said he felt good all over. What did he feel good about?
    A. He felt good because his hounds were very obedient. The Pritchard boys' hounds would not listen to them.
    B. He felt good that was going through with his bet and acting like a man.
    C. He felt good because he had never seen Rainie looked so excited.
    D. He felt good because he thought his hounds would win the bet and his grandfather would be proud of him.

Multiple Choice Study Guide/Quiz Questions *Where the Red Fern Grows*
Chapters XIII, XIV

1. True or False: Billy refused to pay up on his bet. He said the Pritchards had made up the story about the coon to get his money.
    A. True
    B. False

2. What caused Little Ann to throw up her head and whine?
    A. She caught the coon's scent when a breeze began stirring.
    B. She could sense that Billy was in danger.
    C. She smelled another dog coming near them.
    D. She was sad because she thought Billy was giving up.

3. Where was the coon?
    A. It was in the hayloft of a nearby barn.
    B. It was at the very top of an oak tree.
    C. It was hiding in a hollow gatepost.
    D. It was in a hole under an old stump.

4. True or False: Billy decided he didn't want to kill the old coon because it had lived there such a long time.
    A. True
    B. False

5. Which of the following did **not** happen when Billy asked Rubin to give his money back?
    A. Rubin refused to give the money back.
    B. Billy threatened to tell his grandfather what had happened.
    C. Rubin knocked Billy down and started whipping him in the face with his hat.
    D. Rainie took the money and ran home.

6. What were the dogs doing while the boys were fighting?
    A. They were still looking for the coon.
    B. Old Dan and Little Ann were helping Billy fight off the Pritchard boys.
    C. The Pritchard boys' dog, Old Blue, was fighting with Old Dan and Little Ann.
    D. Billy had sent them home to get help from his father.

7. What happened to Rubin?
    A. The coon bit him and he later died of rabies.
    B. He tripped on a small stick, fell on the axe blade, and died.
    C. He accidentally killed his dog during the fight.
    D. He fell into the river and drowned. Billy didn't know Rubin could not swim.

8. What did Billy do to show his sorrow for the incident?
    A. He named the coon after Rubin.
    B. He planted a red fern near where the accident happened.
    C. He took four coon skins to the Pritchard family.
    D. He put flowers on the grave.

9. What news did Billy's grandfather tell him a few days after the accident?
    A. He told Billy the coats being made from Billy's skins were selling very well. He had been invited to St. Louis to meet the man who bought all of his coon skins.
    B. He told Billy the kennel in Kentucky had invited him to bring the dogs back for a dog show.
    C. He told Billy he was traveling to Talequah for supplies. He wanted Billy to go with him.
    D. He told Billy he had entered Old Dan and Little Ann in a championship coon hunting contest.

10. Who went on the trip?
    A. Grandpa, Papa, Billy, and the dogs went.
    B. Only Grandpa and Billy went.
    C. Only Billy and the dogs went.
    D. Papa, Billy, and the dogs went.

Multiple Choice Study Guide/Quiz Questions *Where the Red Fern Grows*
Chapters XV, XVI

1. What "first" happened on the trip that made Billy feel more grown up?
    A. He was allowed to stand watch over the camp during the night.
    B. His grandfather gave him a cup of coffee.
    C. His father offered him a cigarette.
    D. His grandfather let him drive the buggy.

2. Which contest did Billy enter first, and what was the result?
    A. He entered both dogs in an obedience contest. They won second place and red ribbons.
    B. He entered Little Ann in a beauty contest. She won first place and a small silver cup.
    C. He entered Old Dan in a swimming contest. He won first place and a gold medal.
    D. He entered a whooping and hollering contest. He came in third and got a very sore throat.

3. True or False: On their first night of hunting, Billy thought they should go far down river out of range of where the others had gone.
    A. True
    B. False

4. Where did the hounds run the first coon, and what was the result?
    A. They ran it into the river and it got away from them. They were behind in the contest.
    B. They ran it up a nearby tree. Billy was able to get it down by shaking a branch at it. The hounds had an easy kill.
    C. They ran the coon near the camp. The men doused all of the fires and the coon ran straight through the camp.
    D. They ran it so far up the road that another pair of hounds caught it and killed it. They got the credit for the kill.

5. How many coons did the dogs kill on their first night of competition?
    A. They killed five coons.
    B. They killed one coon.
    C. They killed two coons.
    D. They killed three coons.

6. What about the dogs surprised the judge?
    A. He was surprised that they had so much energy, because they were so little.
    B. He was surprised they didn't fight with each other. He said most male/female pairs had ongoing battles while hunting.
    C. He was surprised that the dogs were able to find the scent when the coon had gone so far out on the river bottoms.
    D. He was surprised that they seemed to understand so much of what Billy said to them.

7. Why did one of the hunters come around with a small box in his hands?
    A. He was asking for food donations for the big party at the end of the contest.
    B. He was collecting money for a jackpot for the winner.
    C. He had found the box and wanted to locate the owner.
    D. He was a woodworker. He was selling the boxes as souvenirs.

8. True or False: Billy wanted to go back to the swamp on the final night. The area was the same distance from the mountains and the river, and he thought he would have a better chance of catching a lot of coons.
    A. True
    B. False

9. The judge saw the two hounds stop and stare at Billy at the beginning of the hunt. What was Billy's explanation for their actions?
    A. He said they were waiting for directions on which way to go.
    B. He said they were asking how many hunters were coming.
    C. He said they always liked to look at him and get his scent before they went hunting.
    D. He said he could feel that they knew the hunt was important.

10. After the dogs killed the coon, what did they do that surprised the judge?
    A. They licked and doctored each other's wounds.
    B. Each of the dogs refused to eat until the other had been fed.
    C. They jumped up on Billy and wagged their tails after the hunt was finished.
    D. The hounds would only let Billy pet them. They growled whenever anyone else got near them.

Multiple Choice Study Guide/Quiz Questions *Where the Red Fern Grows*
Chapters XVII-XVIII

1. What was the weather like on this part of the hunt?
    A. There was a hurricane starting up.
    B. It was very cold, but clear.
    C. There was a sleet storm. It was cold and icy.
    D. There was a blizzard, with about a foot of snow.

2. The judge said he thought they should all go back to camp, and leave the dogs where they were. Billy refused to leave his dogs. He said they would die before they would leave a coon in a tree. What did they all finally do?
    A. Only Billy stayed.
    B. They all stayed.
    C. Billy and his grandfather stayed. The others went back to camp.
    D. Billy, his father, and his grandfather stayed. The judge went back to camp.

3. Which of the following did **not** happen to Billy's grandfather?
    A. He caught his foot in a hidden steel trap.
    B. He was unconscious from the pain.
    C. Little Ann found him.
    D. Papa and the judge carried him to a nearby gully and made him as comfortable as possible.

4. What did they do after they had taken care of Grandpa?
    A. They stayed with him to make sure he was all right.
    B. Billy stayed with him while his father and the judge went to the camp for help.
    C. They returned their attention to the dogs and the coon hunt.
    D. They began making a stretcher from branches so they could carry Grandpa back to camp.

5. What did the dogs do?
    A. They ran back to camp.
    B. They took off into the swamp after a new coon.
    C. They lay down near Grandpa's feet and went to sleep.
    D. They went in the direction to which Billy had pointed.

6. True or False: Half of the hunters took Grandpa back to camp to the doctor. The others went with Billy, his father, and the judge to find the dogs.
    A. True
    B. False

7. What happened to the dogs?
    A. They had a severe case of frostbite and had to be taken back to camp.
    B. They fell asleep under the tree and the coon escaped.
    C. They killed the coon after the men thawed them out.
    D. They lost the coon's scent because of the heavy sleet.

8. True or False: Another hunter won first prize. He gave the cup and the money to Billy anyway because Billy and his dogs had been so brave.
    A. True
    B. False

9. Which of the following events did **not** happen when Billy and his father arrived home?
    A. Billy gave the two older girls the small silver cup.
    B. He gave the large gold cup to the youngest girl.
    C. He gave the box of money to his mother.
    D. He asked his mother to give part of the money to his grandfather.

10. What did Billy see his mother doing as he was preparing for bed?
    A. He saw his mother counting the money and making pencil marks on a piece of paper.
    B. He saw his mother feed the dogs and then pray in front of them.
    C. He saw her polish the two cups and put them on the mantel.
    D. He saw her hug his father and heard her say she was glad to see him.

Multiple Choice Study Guide/Quiz Questions *Where the Red Fern Grows*
Chapters XIX-XX

1. What animal did Billy think the dogs had treed the night they went to the Cyclone Timber country?
    A. He thought they had treed a bobcat.
    B. He thought they had treed the ghost coon again.
    C. He thought they had treed a mountain lion.
    D. He thought they had treed a bear cub.

2. How did Billy feel about the animal the dogs had treed?
    A. He was glad they had treed it.
    B. He was not glad that they had treed it.

3. What unusual actions did Old Dan take?
    A. He sat at the base of the tree and whined.
    B. He jumped on Little Ann's back and tried to climb the tree.
    C. He put his tail between his legs and ran away from the tree.
    D. He curled back his lips, snarled, and then growled.

4. What animal had the dogs actually treed?
    A. It was a black bear.
    B. It was a bobcat.
    C. It was a mountain lion.
    D. It was a very large rattlesnake.

5. How did the animal die?
    A. Old Dan bit it in the throat and it bled to death.
    B. Billy sank the axe blade into its back.
    C. Little Ann slashed its belly open.
    D. The dogs chased it to a cliff. It fell over and drowned in the river below.

6. How did Billy feel about what his dogs had done?
    A. He was proud and grateful.
    B. He was angry because they had challenged the other animal.
    C. He was mostly afraid that they were hurt.
    D. He was too numb to feel anything.

7. What did Billy discover about Old Dan as they were walking home?
    A. Old Dan had a broken leg.
    B. Old Dan had a severe head wound.
    C. The other animal had gouged Old Dan's eyes out and he was blind.
    D. Old Dan's belly had been slashed and his entrails were falling out.

8. What happened to the dogs?
    A. Old Dan died. Little Ann stayed with Billy.
    B. Old Dan lived. Little Ann ran away.
    C. Old Dan died. Then Little Ann died on Old Dan's grave.
    D. They both lived, but they were crippled and never hunted again.

9. True or False: Billy's parents told him they were going to use the money he had made to open a kennel for hunting dogs.
    A. True
    B. False

10. According to an old Indian legend, what was the significance of the red fern?
    A. Any spot where the red fern grew was sacred.
    B. The fern grew on a spot where blood had been shed.
    C. The first person to see it would never return to that spot again.
    D. Whoever lived on the land where the fern grew would have good luck in life.

ANSWER KEY-MULTIPLE CHOICE QUIZ/STUDY GUIDE QUESTIONS
Where the Red Fern Grows

Chapters I, II, III, IV
1. A True
2. B
3. A
4. B False
5. D
6. A
7. D
8. B
9. C
10. A

Chapters V, VI, VIII
1. D
2. A
3. B
4. C
5. A True
6. B False
7. D
8. B
9. C
10. A

Chapters VIII, IX
1. D
2. B
3. A True
4. A
5. A
6. B
7. D
8. C
9. C
10. D

Chapters X, XI, XII
1. A
2. C
3. D
4. B
5. B False
6. C
7. A
8. B
9. B False
10. C

Chapters XIII, XIV
1. B False
2. A
3. C
4. A True
5. D
6. C
7. B
8. D
9. D
10. A

Chapters XV, XVI
1. B
2. B
3. A True
4. C
5. D
6. C
7. B
8. A
9. D
10. A

Chapters XVII, XVIII
1. C
2. B
3. D
4. C
5. D
6. A True
7. C
8. B False
9. D
10. B

Chapters XIX, XX
1. A
2. B
3. D
4. C
5. B
6. A
7. D
8. C
9. B False
10. A

PREREADING VOCABULARY WORKSHEETS

Vocabulary Chapters I, II, III, IV
Part I: Using Prior Knowledge and Context Clues
Below are the sentences in which the vocabulary words appear in the text. Read the sentence. Use any clues you can find in the sentence combined with your prior knowledge, and write what you think the underlined words mean on the lines provided.

1. It was too much for him and he took off down the street, *squalling* like a scalded cat.

   _____

2. I kept *coaxing*. On his stomach, an inch at a time, he came to me and laid his head in my hand.

   _____

3. It's strange indeed how memories can lie *dormant* in a man's mind for so many years.

   _____

4. I figured something *drastic* must have happened in his life, as it is very unusual for a hound to be traveling all alone.

   _____

5. Water from a rain puddle or a mountain stream would *quench* his thirst and cool his hot dry throat.

   _____

6. It starts *gnawing* on his heart, and gets all mixed up in his dreams.

   _____

7. I *mulled* them over in my mind.

   _____

8. Next, I went to the barn and up in the loft. Far back over the hay and up under the *eaves*, I hid my can.

   _____

9. After leaving the mountain stream, my *pace* was much slower.

   _____

10. Feeling the *pangs* of hunger gnawing at my stomach, I decided I would stop and eat at the next stream I found.

   _____

Part II: Determining the Meaning Match the vocabulary words to their dictionary definitions.

_____ 1. squalling   A. persuading by pleading or flattery
_____ 2. coaxing   B. severe or radical in nature; extreme
_____ 3. dormant   C. afflicting or worrying persistently
_____ 4. drastic   D. overhang at the edge of a roof
_____ 5. quench   E. sudden sharp spasms of pain
_____ 6. gnawing   F. screaming or crying loudly
_____ 7. mulled   G. inactive but capable of being activated
_____ 8. eaves   H. to satisfy
_____ 9. pace   I. gone over extensively
_____ 10. pangs   J. rate of speed for walking or running

Vocabulary Chapters V, VI, VII
Part I: Using Prior Knowledge and Context Clues
Below are the sentences in which the vocabulary words appear in the text. Read the sentence. Use any clues you can find in the sentence combined with your prior knowledge, and write what you think the underlined words mean on the lines provided.

1. On arriving at the *depot*, my nerve failed me.
   _____

2. They would *waddle* up to the front of the cave, look at the fire, and come scampering back to roll and play in the soft leaves.
   _____

3. With the *hampering* help of my sisters I made the little doghouse.
   _____

4. Now that I had the pups another *obstacle* had cropped up.
   _____

5. It was no use. I just couldn't catch the *wiley* coons.
   _____

6. In desperation I went to my grandfather. He smiled as he listened to my tale of *woe*.
   _____

7. "You know," he said, "a coon has more than one *peculiarity* about him."
   _____

8. "My goodness," Mama said, "you wouldn't think anything so small would be so *vicious.*"
   _____

9. Sometimes he would come out of the water by catching the *dangling* limbs or a leaning birch and climbing up, never touching the bank.

_____

Part II: Determining the Meaning   Match the vocabulary words to their dictionary definitions.

____ 1. depot
____ 2. waddle
____ 3. hampering
____ 4. obstacle
____ 5. wiley
____ 6. woe
____ 7. peculiarity
____ 8. vicious
____ 9. dangling

A. cunning or trickery
B. marked by an aggressive disposition; savage
C. to walk with short steps that tilt the body
D. a railroad or bus station
E. hanging loosely or swinging
F. a notable or distinctive feature or characteristic
G. deep distress or misery
H. preventing free movement or action
I. something that opposes or holds up progress

Vocabulary Chapters VIII-IX
Part I: Using Prior Knowledge and Context Clues
Below are the sentences in which the vocabulary words appear in the text. Read the sentence. Use any clues you can find in the sentence combined with your prior knowledge, and write what you think the underlined words mean on the lines provided.

1. He just lay there in the sunshine, all stretched out and *limber* as a rag.

   _____

2. I heard the *baying* of a hound.

   _____

3. I was expecting one of them to *bawl,* but when it came it startled me.

   _____

4. Like a king in its *domain,* it towered far above the smaller trees.

   _____

5. "If that tree takes a *notion* to fall, it'll mash you flatter than a tadpole's tail."

   _____

6. He showed his sympathy by *nuzzling* me with his head.

   _____

7. In a *sober* voice, he said, "I don't know, Billy."

   _____

Part II: Determining the Meaning   Match the vocabulary words to their dictionary definitions.

____ 1. limber   A. to cry or wail loudly
____ 2. baying   B. territory over which rule or control is exercised
____ 3. bawl   C. serious, grave, or solemn
____ 4. domain   D. uttering a deep. prolonged bark
____ 5. notion   E. bending or flexing readily; pliable
____ 6. nuzzling   F. rubbing or pushing against gently with the nose
____ 7. sober   G. an idea or conception

Vocabulary Chapters X, XI, XII
Part I: Using Prior Knowledge and Context Clues
Below are the sentences in which the vocabulary words appear in the text. Read the sentence. Use any clues you can find in the sentence combined with your prior knowledge, and write what you think the underlined words mean on the lines provided.

1. The next morning I hung around the house for a while, and then *nonchalantly* whistled my way out to the barn.

   _____

2. He strutted around with a *belligerent* and tough attitude.

   _____

3. I came to a point where a *slough* of crystal-clear water ran into the river.

   _____

4. I had often wondered what Old Dan would do if Little Ann got into some kind of a *predicament.*

   _____

5. "No, you won't," said Grandpa. "Come on, I'm going to lock up." *Begrudgingly*, they walked out.

   _____

Part II: Determining the Meaning   Match the vocabulary words to their dictionary definitions.

   ____ 1. nonchalantly   A. hostile or aggressive; inclined to fight
   ____ 2. belligerent   B. unpleasant or troublesome situation
   ____ 3. slough   C. unconcernedly or indifferently
   ____ 4. predicament   D. reluctantly
   ____ 5. begrudgingly   E. a depression or hollow, usually filled with mud

Vocabulary Chapters XIII-XIV
Part I: Using Prior Knowledge and Context Clues
Below are the sentences in which the vocabulary words appear in the text. Read the sentence. Use any clues you can find in the sentence combined with your prior knowledge, and write what you think the underlined words mean on the lines provided.

1. Just then I heard growling, and a *commotion* off to one side.

   _____

2. Rainie had been so *dazed* when he got home, they couldn't make out what he was trying to tell them, but they knew it must have been something bad.

   _____

3. I was *dumbfounded*. I said, "All right with me? Why, Grandpa, you know it's all right with me, but what do I have to do with it?"

   _____

4. Back in her chair, she *gloated* over the others. "You just wait and see," she said. "It'll be all mine, nobody's but mine, and I'll put my banty eggs in it."

   _____

5. Knowing that Papa and I would be gone for several days, I did everything I could to make things *convenient* for Mama.

   _____

6. Just when I thought we were ready to leave, Grandma came *bustling* out.

   _____

Part II: Determining the Meaning   Match the vocabulary words to their dictionary definitions.

_____ 1. commotion   A. stunned, stupefied
_____ 2. dazed   B. easy to reach; accessible
_____ 3. dumbfounded   C. moving energetically and busily
_____ 4. gloated   D. filled with astonishment and perplexity
_____ 5. convenient   E. expressed great pleasure or self-satisfaction
_____ 6. bustling   F. an agitated disturbance

Vocabulary Chapters XV-XVI

Part I: Using Prior Knowledge and Context Clues

Below are the sentences in which the vocabulary words appear in the text. Read the sentence. Use any clues you can find in the sentence combined with your prior knowledge, and write what you think the underlined words mean on the lines provided.

1. With an *astonished* look on his face, Grandpa exclaimed, "Well, I'll be darned."

   _____

2. An *eerie* screech from a tree close by made shivers run up and down my spine.

   _____

3. His body was stiff and straight, his head high in the air, his large muscles *quivered* and jerked under his glassy coat, but something went wrong.

   _____

4. Grandpa very *gingerly* started picking his way. His tender old feet moved from one smooth rock to another.

   _____

5. We could tell they were coming so we *doused* all the fires and, sure enough, they came right through camp.

   _____

Part II: Determining the Meaning
Match the vocabulary words to their dictionary definitions.

_____ 1.	astonished	A.	strange and frightening
_____ 2.	eerie	B.	put out; extinguished
_____ 3.	quivered	C.	filled with sudden wonder or amazement
_____ 4.	gingerly	D.	shook with a slight, rapid movement
_____ 5.	doused	E.	with great care or delicacy; cautious

Vocabulary Chapters XVII-XVIII
Part I: Using Prior Knowledge and Context Clues
Below are the sentences in which the vocabulary words appear in the text. Read the sentence. Use any clues you can find in the sentence combined with your prior knowledge, and write what you think the underlined words mean on the lines provided.

1. Once during a momentary *lull* of the storm, I thought I heard the baying of a hound.

   _____

2. Old Dan was treed down in a deep *gully*. I slid off the bank and ran to him.

   _____

3. Papa *notched* the old snag so it would fall away from our fire.

   _____

4. Old Dan made a *lunge*.

   _____

5. "It's not, either," the little one piped in a *defiant* voice.

   _____

6. Turning her back to us, she walked over and set it on the *mantel.*

   _____

7. Just when they were on the *verge* of sawing it in two, so each would have her allotted share, Papa settled the squabble by giving the oldest one a silver dollar.

   _____

8. Just when they were on the verge of sawing it in two, so each would have her allotted share, Papa settled the *squabble* by giving the oldest one a silver dollar.

   _____

Part II: Determining the Meaning   Match the vocabulary words to their dictionary definitions.

_____ 1. lull
_____ 2. gully
_____ 3. notched
_____ 4. lunge
_____ 5. defiant
_____ 6. mantel
_____ 7. verge
_____ 8. squabble

A. a relatively calm interval
B. a noisy quarrel, usually about a trivial matter
C. boldly resistant
D. a deep ditch or channel
E. a sudden forward movement or plunge
F. the point beyond which an action is likely to begin
G. made a V-shaped cut
H. the protruding shelf over a fireplace

Vocabulary Chapters XIX-XX
Part I: Using Prior Knowledge and Context Clues
Below are the sentences in which the vocabulary words appear in the text. Read the sentence. Use any clues you can find in the sentence combined with your prior knowledge, and write what you think the underlined words mean on the lines provided.

1. The only good I could see in killing one was getting rid of a vicious *predatory* animal.

   _____

2. I went *berserk*, and charged into the fight.

   _____

3. The long, *lithe* body dipped low to the ground.

   _____

4. The *keen* edge cleaved through the tough skin.

   _____

5. The keen edge *cleaved* through the tough skin.

   _____

6. It was the end of the trail for the *scourge* of the mountains.

   _____

7. In his dying convulsions the axe had become *dislodged* from the wound.

   _____

8. I thought perhaps she had a wound I had overlooked. I felt and *probed* with my fingers.

   _____

9. I felt its warm *caress* as it fanned my face.

_____

Part II: Determining the Meaning Match the vocabulary words to their dictionary definitions.

_____ 1. predatory   A. destructively or frenetically violent
_____ 2. berserk   B. source of widespread, dreadful devastation
_____ 3. lithe   C. living by hunting other organisms
_____ 4. keen   D. a gentle touch showing fondness or love
_____ 5. cleaved   E. marked by effortless grace
_____ 6. scourge   F. removed or forced out
_____ 7. dislodged   G. pierced or penetrated
_____ 8. probed   H. explored; investigated
_____ 9. caress   I. having a fine, sharp cutting edge or point

ANSWER KEY-PREREADING VOCABULARY WORKSHEETS
Where the Red Fern Grows

Chapters I, II, III, IV
1. F
2. A
3. G
4. B
5. H
6. C
7. I
8. D
9. J
10. E

Chapters V, VI, VII
1. D
2. C
3. H
4. I
5. A
6. G
7. F
8. B
9. E

Chapters VIII, IX
1. E
2. D
3. A
4. B
5. G
6. F
7. C

Chapters X, XI, XII
1. C
2. A
3. E
4. B
5. D

Chapters XIII, XIV
1. F
2. A
3. D
4. E
5. B
6. C

Chapters XV, XVI
1. C
2. A
3. D
4. E
5. B

Chapters XVII, XVIII
1. A
2. D
3. G
4. E
5. C
6. H
7. F
8. B

Chapters XIX, XX
1. C
2. A
3. E
4. I
5. G
6. B
7. F
8. H
9. D

DAILY LESSONS

LESSON ONE

Objectives

    1. To introduce the *Where the Red Fern Grows* unit
    2. To relate students' prior knowledge to the new material
    3. To distribute books and other related materials (study guides, reading assignments)
    4. To do the prereading work for Chapters I-IV

Activity #1

    Make a bulletin board display of pictures of people with their pets. Make sure to include pictures of children, especially boys between the ages of ten and fourteen. Title the board *People and Pets-A Special Relationship*. Also show pictures of the Ozark mountains, hunting dogs, and raccoons. First discuss pets. Ask students to share information about their own pets and the kinds of things they like to do with them. Then ask students to tell you what they know about the Ozarks and hunting, about Wilson Rawls, and about the novel. Tell them the novel they will be reading is set in the Ozark Mountains, and is about a boy and his dogs. Do the included group KWL sheet with the students. Put any information the students know in the K column (What I Know.) Ask students what they want to find out and put that information in the W column (What I Want to Find Out.) Keep the sheet and refer to it while reading. After reading the novel, complete the L column (What I Learned.)

Activity #2

    Distribute the materials students will use in this unit. Explain in detail how students are to use these materials.

    Study Guides Students should preview the study guide questions before each reading assignment to get a feeling for what events and ideas are important in that section. After reading the section, students will (as a class or individually) answer the questions to review the important events and ideas from that section of the book. Students should keep the study guides as study materials for the unit test.

    Reading Assignment Sheet You need to fill in the reading assignment sheet to let students know when their reading has to be completed. You can either write the assignment sheet on a side blackboard or bulletin board and leave it there for students to see each day, or you can "ditto" copies for each student to have. In either case, you should advise students to become very familiar with the reading assignments so they know what is expected of them.

    Extra Activities Center The unit resource portion of this unit contains suggestions for a library of related books and articles in your classroom as well as crossword and word search puzzles.

Make an extra activities center in your room where you will keep these materials for students to use. (Bring the books and articles in from the library and keep several copies of the puzzles on hand.) Explain to students that these materials are available for students to use when they finish reading assignments or other class work early.

<u>Books</u> Each school has its own rules and regulations regarding student use of school books. Advise students of the procedures that are normal for your school.

<u>Activity #3</u>

Show students how to preview the study questions and do the vocabulary work for Chapters I-IV of *Where the Red Fern Grows*. If students do not finish this assignment in class, they should complete it prior to the next class meeting.

KWL *Where the Red Fern Grows*

Directions: Before reading, think about what you already know about Wilson Rawls and/or *Where the Red Fern Grows*. Write the information in the K column. Think about what you would like to find out from reading the book. Write your questions in the W column. After you have read the book, use the L column to write the answers to your questions from the W column, and anything else you remember from the book.

K What I Know	W What I Want to Find Out	L What I Learned

LESSON TWO

Objectives
1. To read Chapters I-IV
2. To review the main ideas and events from Chapters I-IV
3. To introduce the Nonfiction assignment

Activity #1

You may want to read Chapter I aloud to the students to set the mood for the novel. Invite willing students to read Chapters II, III, and IV aloud to the rest of the class.

Activity #2

Give the students time to answer the study guide questions, and then discuss the answers in detail. Write the answers on the board or overhead projector so students can have the correct answers for study purposes. Encourage students to take notes. If the students own their books, encourage them to use high lighter pens to mark important passages and the answers to the study guide questions.

Note: It is a good practice in public speaking and leadership skills for individuals students to take charge of leading the discussion of the study questions. Perhaps a different student could go to the front of the class and lead the discussion each day that the study questions are discussed during this unit. Of course, the teacher should guide the discussion when appropriate and be sure to fill in any gaps the students leave.

Activity #3

Distribute copies of the Nonfiction Assignment sheet and go over it in detail with the students. Give them the due date for the assignment (Lesson 19.) Some suggestions for the assignment are pros and cons on hunting as a sport, raising hound dogs, the relationship between a person and a pet, and life in the Ozark mountains.

NONFICTION ASSIGNMENT SHEET *Where the Red Fern Grows*
(To be completed after reading the required nonfiction article)

Name _____ Date _____ Class _____

Title of Nonfiction Read _____

Written By _____ Publication Date _____

I. Factual Summary: Write a short summary of the piece you read.

II. Vocabulary:
    1. With which vocabulary words in the piece did you encounter some degree of difficulty?

    2. How did you resolve your lack of understanding with these words?

III. Interpretation: What was the main point the author wanted you to get from reading his/her work?

IV. Criticism:
    1. With which points of the piece did you agree or find easy to accept? Why?

    2. With which points of the piece did you disagree or find difficult to believe? Why?

V. Personal Response: What do you think about this piece? OR How does this piece influence your ideas?

LESSON THREE

Objectives
> 1. To do the prereading and vocabulary work for chapters V-VII
> 2. To read Chapters V-VII
> 3. To evaluate students' oral reading

Activity #1

Give students about fifteen minutes to preview the study questions for Chapters V-VII and do the related vocabulary work.

Activity #2

Have students read chapters V-VII of *Where the Red Fern Grows* out loud in class. You probably know the best way to get readers with your class; pick students at random, ask for volunteers, or use whatever method works best for your group. Since much of the book is written in dialog, you may want to have different students read the parts of the characters, and also the narrator. If you have not yet completed an oral reading evaluation for your students for this marking period, this would be a good opportunity to do so. A form is included with this unit for your convenience. If students do not complete reading Chapters V-VII in class, they should do so prior to your next class meeting.

LESSON FOUR

Objectives
> 1. To check students' understanding of the main ideas and events from Chapters I-VII
> 2. To preview the study questions for Chapters VIII-IX
> 3. To familiarize students with the vocabulary in Chapters VIII-IX
> 4. To read Chapters VIII-IX

Activity #1

Quiz--distribute quizzes (multiple choice study questions for Chapters I-VII) and give students about ten minutes to complete them. Have students exchange papers. Grade the quizzes as a class. Collect the papers for recording the grades.

Activity #2

Give students about fifteen minutes to preview the study questions for Chapters VIII-IX and do the related vocabulary work.

Activity #3

Have students read Chapters VIII-IX for the rest of the period. If you have not completed the oral reading evaluations, do so now. If the evaluations have been completed, you may want the students to read silently. If students do not complete the reading assignment in class, they should do so prior to your next class meeting.

ORAL READING EVALUATION *Where the Red Fern Grows*

Name_____Class_____Date _____--

SKILL	EXCELLENT	GOOD	AVERAGE	FAIR	POOR
Fluency	5	4	3	2	1
Clarity	5	4	3	2	1
Audibility	5	4	3	2	1
Pronunciation	5	4	3	2	1
_____	5	4	3	2	1
_____	5	4	3	2	1

Total _____ Grade _____

Comments:

LESSON FIVE

Objectives
    1. To give students the opportunity to practice writing a classified ad
    2. To give the teacher the opportunity to evaluate each student's writing skills

Activity #1

    Distribute Writing Assignment #1 and discuss the directions in detail. Allow the remaining class time for students to work on the assignment. Give students an additional two or three days to complete the assignment, if necessary.

Activity #2

    Distribute copies of the Writing Evaluation Form that is included in this Unit Plan. Explain to students that during Lesson Nine you will be holding individual writing conferences about this writing assignment. Make sure they are familiar with the criteria on the Writing Evaluation Form.

Follow-Up: After you have graded the assignments, have a writing conference with each student, (This unit schedules one in Lesson Nine.) After the writing conference, allow students to revise their papers using your suggestions to complete the revision. I suggest grading the revisions on an A-C-E scale (all revisions well-done, some revisions made, few or no revisions made.) This will speed your grading time and still give some credit for the students' efforts.

LESSON SIX

Objectives
    1. To review the main ideas and events in Chapters VIII-IX
    2. To preview the study questions and vocabulary for Chapters X-XII
    3. To read Chapters X-XII silently

Activity #1

    Ask students to get out their books and some paper but not their study guides. Tell students to write down ten questions and answers which cover the main events and ideas in Chapters VIII-IX. Discuss the students' questions and answers orally, making a list on the board of the questions with brief responses. Put a star next to students' questions and answers that are essentially the same as the study guide questions. Be sure that all of the study guide questions are answered.

Activity #2

    Give students about 15 minutes to do the prereading and vocabulary work for Chapters X-XII.

Activity #3

    Give students the remainder of the period to begin silently reading Chapters X-XII. Remind them that the reading must be completed prior to your next class meeting.

WRITING ASSIGNMENT 1 *Where the Red Fern Grows*

PROMPT

Billy found the answer he wanted in an advertisement in an old newspaper. He read about a kennel in Kentucky that was selling hunting dogs.

Your assignment is to write a classified ad for a newspaper. It should tell what you want to sell, how much it costs, and how to contact you.

PREWRITING

The first thing you need to do is read some classified ads to get and idea of the kinds of things you can sell and how to write an ad. Decide what you want to sell. You could sell kittens, puppies, baby rabbits, or other domestic animals. You might want to sell an outgrown bicycle, a video game system, or some athletic equipment.

DRAFTING

Follow the format of the ads you looked at. Write a fairly detailed description of the item you are selling. Include its age, size, and physical condition. Mention any special attributes that may be good selling points. Then tell your asking price and how to get in touch with you.

PROMPT

When you finish the rough draft of your classified ad, ask another student to read it. After reading your rough draft, he/she should tell you what he/she liked best about your work, which parts were difficult to understand, and ways in which your work could be improved. Reread your paper considering your critic's comments, and make the corrections you think are necessary.

PROOFREADING

Do a final proofreading of your paper, double-checking your grammar, spelling, organization, and the clarity of your ideas.

WRITING EVALUATION FORM *Where the Red Fern Grows*

Name _____ Date _____ Class _____

Writing Assignment #1 for *Where the Red Fern Grows*

Circle One For Each Item:

<u>Introduction</u>	excellent	good	fair	poor
<u>Body Paragraphs</u>	excellent	good	fair	poor
<u>Summary</u>	excellent	good	fair	poor
<u>Grammar</u>	excellent	good	fair	poor (errors noted)
<u>Spelling</u>	excellent	good	fair	poor (errors noted)
<u>Punctuation</u>	excellent	good	fair	poor (errors noted)
<u>Legibility</u>	excellent	good	fair	poor (errors noted)

Strengths:

Weaknesses:

Comments/Suggestions:

LESSON SEVEN

Objectives
    1. To review the main ideas and events from Chapters X-XII
    2. To preview the study questions and vocabulary for Chapters XIII-XIV
    3. To read Chapters XIII-XIV

Activity #1
    Review the study guide questions and answers for Chapters X-XII.

Activity #2
    Give students about fifteen minutes to complete the prereading and vocabulary work for Chapters XIII-XIV.

Activity #3
    Depending on the needs of your group, have the students read these chapters orally or silently. Remind them that any reading not completed in class must be finished before the next class meeting.

LESSON EIGHT

Objectives
    1. To review the main ideas and events from Chapters XIII-XIV
    2. To give students the opportunity to practice writing a persuasive argument

Activity #1
    Go over the study guide questions and answers with students. Tell them they will have a quiz on Chapters VIII-XIV the class period after the writing conference.

Activity #2
    Distribute Writing Assignment #2. Discuss the directions in detail and give students ample time to complete the assignment.

LESSON NINE

Objectives
    1. To have students revise their first writing assignment papers
    2. To work on other assignments independently

Activity #1
    Call students to your desk or some other private area to discuss their papers from Writing Assignment #1. Use the completed Writing Evaluation Form as a basis for your critique.

Activity #2   Students should use this period (when they are not conferencing with you) to work on their Nonfiction assignment, or to review the study guide questions they have covered so far.

WRITING ASSIGNMENT #2 *Where the Red Fern Grows*

PROMPT

You have wanted a pet for a long time, but your parents have always said no. Now it is almost time for your birthday. Your grades have been very good, and so has your behavior. You decide to ask for a pet one more time. Your assignment is to form a request in favor of having a pet. You will present the request to your parents.

PREWRITING

First, decide what kind of pet you want. Take into consideration the type of home you have, its location, and your family's life style. Then decide what kind of reasons you have for wanting a pet. You may want to have some pictures of cute pets like the one you want. You may also want to have some written statements from friends who have pets, and magazine articles about the benefits of having a pet. Also think about how you will take care of the pet.

DRAFTING

Begin with an introductory paragraph in which you state your request for a pet, and name the kind of pet you want.

In the body of the paper, tell the reasons you want a pet. Tell why the pet fits into your life style. List the advantages to your family of having a pet. Describe in detail how you plan to care for the pet. You may want to include a paragraph that cites research on the value of having a pet. Include another paragraph with quotes from friends and relatives who have pets.

In your summary, restate why you would like to have a pet.

PROMPT

When you finish the rough draft of your paper, ask a student who sits near you to read it. After reading your rough draft, he/she should tell you what he/she liked best about your work, which parts were difficult to understand, and ways in which your work could be improved. Reread your paper considering your critic's comments, and make the corrections you think are necessary.

PROOFREADING

Do a final proofreading of your paper double-checking your grammar, spelling, organization, and the clarity of your ideas.

LESSON TEN

Objectives

    1. To check to see that the students have done the required reading
    2. To complete the prereading and vocabulary work for Chapters XV-XVI
    3. To silently read chapters XV-XVI

Activity #1

    Give students a quiz on Chapters VIII-XIV. Use either the short answer or multiple choice form of the study guide questions as a quiz so that in discussing the answers to the quiz you also answer the study guide questions. Collect the papers for grading.

Activity #2

    Give students about fifteen minutes to preview the study questions and do the related vocabulary work.

Activity #3

    Have students read the chapters silently and answer the study guide questions. Remind students that any work not completed in class must be finished before the next class meeting.

LESSON ELEVEN

Objectives

    1. To give the students the opportunity to practice stating their opinion in writing
    2. To give the teacher the opportunity to evaluate the students' writing skills

Activity

    Distribute Writing Assignment #3. Discuss the directions in detail and give students ample time to complete the assignment.

LESSON TWELVE

Objectives
1. To review the main ideas and events from Chapters XV-XVI
2. To complete the prereading and vocabulary work for Chapters XVII-XVIII
2. To silently read chapters XVII-XVIII

Activity #1
Go over the study guide questions for Chapters XV-XVI.

Activity #2
Give students about fifteen minutes to preview the study questions and do the related vocabulary work for Chapters XVII-XVIII.

Activity #3
Have students read the chapters silently and answer the study guide questions. Remind them that any work not finished in class must be completed before the next class meeting.

WRITING ASSIGNMENT #3 *Where the Red Fern Grows*

PROMPT

Billy's parents wanted to move from their mountain home to the town. His mother said she wanted her children to have more educational opportunities, and to have the chance to meet people. However, Billy enjoyed his life in the Ozark mountains. Which do you prefer: a rural or an urban lifestyle? Your assignment is to state your preference and write about it.

PREWRITING

First, decide which kind of lifestyle you prefer. If you have only lived in one place (an urban or a rural area), try finding people who have lived in another area. Ask them what it was like, and what they liked and disliked about it. Go to the library and read about various places to live. Make lists of the pros and cons of living in each environment.

DRAFTING

Begin with an introductory paragraph in which you state your preference.

In the body of the paper, tell the reasons you want to live in that locale. Describe the place in detail. Describe your activities there. List the advantages of living in the area you have chosen. Include research statistics and testimonial from others who live there. If possible, compare and contrast your chosen area with an opposite locale.

In your summary, restate why you want to live in that particular area.

PROMPT

When you finish the rough draft of your paper, ask a student who sits near you to read it. After reading your rough draft, he/she should tell you what he/she liked best about your work, which parts were difficult to understand, and ways in which your work could be improved. Reread your paper considering your critic's comments, and make the corrections you think are necessary.

PROOFREADING

Do a final proofreading of your paper double-checking your grammar, spelling, organization, and the clarity of your ideas.

LESSON THIRTEEN

Objectives
    1. To review the main ideas and events from Chapters XVII-XVIII
    2. To complete the prereading and vocabulary work for Chapters XIX-XX
    3. To read the chapters silently

Activity #1
    Go over the study guide questions for Chapters XVII-XVIII.

Activity #2
    Give students about fifteen minutes to preview the study questions and do the related vocabulary work for Chapters XIX-XX.

Activity #3
    Have students read the chapters silently. Assign a section for them to practice reading orally for the next class. Tell them they will be doing a dramatic oral reading of the last two chapters.

LESSON FOURTEEN

Objectives
    1. To review the main ideas and events from Chapters XIX-XX
    2. To present a dramatic oral reading from Chapters XIX-XX
    3. To make sure students have the answers to all of the study guide questions

Activity #1
    Go over the study guide questions for Chapters XIX-XX. Remind students to correct any mistakes they have.

Activity #2
    Invite students to take turns reading their assigned parts aloud. Tell the other students they can either follow along in the book or close their eyes and listen attentively.

Activity #3
    Ask students to check through their notes and make sure they have answers for all of the study guide questions. Students who are missing answers should make arrangements with you or another student to get the answers.

LESSON FIFTEEN

Objective
> To discuss *Where the Red Fern Grows* at the interpretive and critical levels

Activity #1
> Choose the questions from the Extra Writing Assignments/Discussion Questions which seem most appropriate for your students. A class discussion of these questions is most effective if students have been given the opportunity to formulate answers to the questions prior to the discussion. To this end, you may either have all the students formulate answers to all the questions, divide the class into groups and assign one or more questions to each group, or you could assign one question to each student in your class. The option you choose will make a difference in the amount of class time needed for this activity.

Activity #2
> After students have had ample time to formulate answers to the questions, begin your class discussion of the questions and the ideas presented by the questions. Be sure students take notes during the discussion so they have information to study for the unit test.

LESSON SIXTEEN

Objective
> To give students time in the library to work on their nonfiction assignments

Activity
> Take the class to the library to work on their nonfiction assignment. Students who have completed it can review for the test or read another novel silently.

EXTRA WRITING ASSIGNMENT /DISCUSSION QUESTIONS
Where the Red Fern Grows

Interpretive

1. From what point of view is the novel written? How does this affect your understanding of the story?

2. Discuss the main themes in the novel.

3. Discuss Billy's growth and maturation from the age of ten through fourteen.

4. How does the introduction in Chapter I set the tone for the novel? Was it effective?

5. Discuss the symbolism of the red fern.

6. What did Billy's actions in obtaining the dogs tell you about his character?

7. What did Billy's actions on his first hunting trip tell you about his character?

8. Why did Billy keep checking the lantern handle in the days following Little Ann's rescue?

9. Why did Old Dan growl at the mountain lion? Do you think he remembered their first encounter with a mountain lion when Billy was bringing the puppies home from Talequah?

10. Why didn't the narrator name any of the human characters in the story? (Mama, Papa, and Grandpa are really titles, not given names.)

11. Do you think Grandpa made a wise choice in agreeing to the Pritchards' bet? Why or why not? What would you have done in a similar circumstance?

12. What was Grandpa's role in Billy's life? Was he a good role model for Billy?

13. The narrator says he never returned to the Ozarks after he moved away. Why do you suppose this was so?

14. Compare and contrast Billy's feelings for his home in the mountains with that of his parents.

15. Early in the novel, the narrator describes Old Dan as being the aggressive one and Little Ann as being the smart one. Give examples of the way that the writer shows this to be true.

Critical

16. Which of the characters were best defined? Give examples from the novel.

17. Discuss the role of religion in the novel.

18. Was Rawls' portrayal of a boy's life in the Ozark mountains effective?

19. Which of the events were most believable?

20. Which events did you find hard to believe? Why?

21. Was the use of flashback effective in the presentation of the novel?

22. Was the dogs' death important to the story? Why or why not?

23. Discuss the use of foreshadowing in the novel.

24. Was the use of first person narrative effective in the presentation of the novel? Why or why not?

Personal Response

25. Which of the characters did you like, and why?

26. Which of the characters did you dislike, and why?

27. Which scene in the story did you like most? Why?

28. Was the title effective? Why or why not?

29. What other title would you choose for this book?

30. Would you recommend this book to a friend? Why or why not?

31. Did you like the ending of the novel? Why or why not?

32. What do you think Billy will do next?

33. Did you expect the red fern to be mentioned more frequently, or at an earlier point in the novel? Why or why not?

QUOTATIONS *Where the Red Fern Grows*

Discuss the significance of the following quotations.

1. It's strange indeed how memories can lie dormant in a man's mind for so many years. Yet those memories can be awakened and brought forth fresh and new, just by something you've seen, or something you've heard, or the sight of an old familiar face.

2. I suppose there's a time in practically every young boy's life wen he's affected by that wonderful disease of puppy love.

3. I thought this was wonderful. I'd finally grown up to be a man. I was going to help Papa with the farm.

4. Right now there was something more important-fifty dollars-a fabulous sum-a fortune-far more money than I had ever seen. Somehow, some way, I was determined to have it.

5. In a quavering voice, he said, "Well, son, it's your money. You worked for it, and you worked hard. You got it honestly, and you want some dogs. We're going to get those dogs. Be darned! Be darned!"

6. I couldn't understand these townspeople. If they weren't staring at a fellow, they were laughing at him.

7. I heard him mutter, "There's not a one in that bunch with that kind of grit."

8. The blood froze in my veins. I was terrified. Although I had never heard one, I knew what it was. It was the scream of a mountain lion.

9. I looked up again at the names carved in the tree. Yes, it was all there like a large puzzle. Piece by piece, each fit perfectly until the puzzle was complete. It could not have happened without the help of an unseen power.

10. Papa said, "Billy, I don't want you to feel badly about the people in town. I don't think they were poking fun at you, anyway not like you think they were."

11. "Billy," he said, "I want you to take a hammer and pull the nails from every one of those traps. It's summertime and their fur isn't any good. Besides, I don't think this is very sportsmanlike. The coon doesn't have a chance. It's all right this time. You needed this one, but from now on I want you to catch them with your own dogs. That way they have a fifty-fifty chance."

12. "It's all over," I said. "There'll be no more sessions. I've worked hard and I've done my best. From now on it's all up to you. Hunting season is just a few days away and I'm going to let you rest for I want you to be in good shape the night it opens."

13. "Billy," she said," I don't approve of this hunting but it looks like I can't say no; not after all you've been through, getting your dogs, and all that training."

14. This was what I had prayed for, worked and sweated for, my own little hounds bawling on the trail of a river coon. I don't know why I cried, but I did. While the tears rolled, I whooped again and again.

15. At that moment, no boy in the world could have been more proud of his dogs than I was. Never again would I doubt them.

16. As our buggy wound its way up through the bottoms, Grandpa started talking. "You know, Billy," he said, "about this tree-chopping of yours, I think it's all right. In fact, I think it would be a good thing if all young boys had to cut down a big tree like that once in their life. It does something for them. It gives them determination and will power. That's a good thing for a man to have. It goes a long way in his life. The American people have a lot of it. They have proved that, all down through history, but they could do with a lot more of it."

17. He stepped over and laid his hand on my shoulder. In a solemn voice, he said, "We won't talk about this again. Now, I want you to forget it ever happened because it wasn't your fault. Oh, I know it's hard for a boy to ever completely forget something like that. All through your life you'll think of it now and then, but try not to let it bother you, and don't ever feel guilty about it. It's not good for a young boy to feel that way."

18. "Yes, sir," he said. "I think we have the best darn coon hounds in these Ozark Mountains, and just as sure as shootin', we're going to win that gold cup."

19. "You know, I've always felt like there was something strange about those dogs. I don't know just what it is, and I can't exactly put my finger on it, yet I can feel it. Maybe it's just my imagination. I don't rightly know."

20. Very seriously, Papa said, "You know, I have two mules down on my place. One is almost as big as a barn. The other one isn't much bigger than a jack rabbit, but that little mule can out pull the big one every time."

21. "Men," said Mr. Kyle, "people have been trying to understand dogs ever since the beginning of time. One never knows what they'll do. You can read every day where a dog saved the life of a drowning child, or lay down his life for his master. Some people call this loyalty. I don't. I may be wrong, but I call it love-the deepest kind of love."

22. "It's a shame that people all over the world can't have that kind of love in their hearts," he said. "There would be no wars, slaughter, or murder; no greed or selfishness. It would be the kind of world that God wants us to have--a wonderful world."

23. Glancing at Old Dan, Papa said, "It's in his blood, Billy. He's a hunting hound, and the best one I ever saw. He only has two loves--you and hunting. That's all he knows."

24. I looked at his grave and, with tears in my eyes, I voiced these words: "You were worth it, old friend, and a thousand times over."

25. "You've done no wrong, Billy," she said. "I know it hurts, but at one time or another, everyone suffers. Even the Good Lord suffered while He was here on earth."

26. "Billy," he said, "there are times in a boy's life when he has to stand up like a man. This is one of those times. I know what you're going through and how it hurts, but there's always an answer. The Good Lord has a reason for everything He does."

LESSON SEVENTEEN

Objective
To review all of the vocabulary work done in this unit

Vocabulary Review Activities

1. Divide your class into two teams and have an old-fashioned spelling or definition bee.

2. Give each of your students (or students in groups of two, three or four) a *Where the Red Fern Grows* Vocabulary Word Search Puzzle. The person (group) to find all of the vocabulary words in the puzzle first wins.

3. Give students a *Where the Red Fern Grows* Vocabulary Word Search Puzzle without the word list. The person or group to find the most vocabulary words in the puzzle wins.

4. Use a *Where the Red Fern Grows* Vocabulary Crossword Puzzle. Put the puzzle onto a transparency on the overhead projector (so everyone can see it), and do the puzzle together as a class.

5. Give students a *Where the Red Fern Grows Vocabulary* Matching Worksheet to do.

6. Divide your class into two teams. Use the *Where the Red Fern Grows* vocabulary words with their letters jumbled as a word list. Student 1 from Team A faces off against Student 1 from Team B. You write the first jumbled word on the board. The first student (1A or 1B) to unscramble the word wins the chance for his/her team to score points. If 1A wins the jumble, go to student 2A and give him/her a definition. He/she must give you the correct spelling of the vocabulary word which fits that definition. If he/she does, Team A scores a point, and you give student 3A a definition for which you expect a correctly spelled matching vocabulary word. Continue giving Team A definitions until some team member makes an incorrect response. An incorrect response sends the game back to the jumbled-word face off, this time with students 2A and 2B. Instead of repeating giving definitions to the first few students of each team, continue with the student after the one who gave the last incorrect response on the team. For example, if Team B wins the jumbled-word face-off, and student 5B gave the last incorrect answer for Team B, you would start this round of definition questions with student 6B, and so on. The team with the most points wins!

7. Have students write a story in which they correctly use as many vocabulary words as possible. Have students read their compositions orally. Post the most original compositions on your bulletin board.

LESSON EIGHTEEN

Objectives
    1. To study in more detail some of the main characters and events in *Where the Red Fern Grows*
    2. To write and present a skit based on the novel

Activity #1
    Divide your class into groups, one for each section of the novel. Have the groups develop a short skit based on that section of the novel. Encourage them to write their own dialog and make simple props from paper or objects in the classroom.

Activity #2
    Have groups present their skits in order according to the sections of the novel.

LESSON NINETEEN

Objectives
    1. To widen the breadth of students' knowledge about the topics discussed or touched upon in *Where the Red Fern Grows*
    2. To check students' non-fiction assignments

Activity
    Ask each student to give a brief oral report about the nonfiction work he/she read for the nonfiction assignment. Your criteria for evaluating this report will vary depending on the level of your students. You may wish for students to give a complete report without using notes of any kind, or you may want students to read directly from a written report, or you may want to do something in between these two extremes. Just make students aware of your criteria in ample time for them to prepare their reports.
    Start with one student's report, After that, ask if anyone else in the class has read on a topic related to the first student's report. If no one has, choose another student at random. After each report, be sure to ask if anyone has a report related to the one just completed. That will help keep a continuity during the discussion of the reports.

LESSON TWENTY

Objectives
1. To watch a movie version of the novel *Where the Red Fern Grows*
2. To compare and contrast the movie with the novel

Activity #1

The movie version of *Where the Red Fern Grows* is available in many video stores, and through educational film distributors. Show the movie in class.

Activity #2

Although the movie closely parallels the book, there are a few differences. Discuss the ways in which the movie and the novel were similar and different. Discuss the reasons for the differences, and the effects they had on the students as viewers. Have students draw a Venn Diagram to record similarities and differences. You may want the students to write a short comparison/contrast paper after this activity.

LESSON TWENTY ONE

Objective
    To review the main ideas presented in *Where the Red Fern Grows*

Activity #1
    Choose one of the review games/activities included in the packet and spend your class period as outlined there.

Activity #2
    Remind students of the date for the Unit Test. Stress the review of the Study Guides and their class notes as a last minute, brush-up review for homework.

REVIEW GAMES / ACTIVITIES

1. Ask the class to make up a unit test for *Where the Red Fern Grows*. The test should have 4 sections: multiple choice, true/false, short answer and essay. Students may use 1/2 period to make the test, including a separate answer sheet, and then swap papers and use the other 1/2 class period to take an open book test a classmate has devised.

2. Take 1/2 period for students to make up true and false questions with answers. Collect the papers and divide the class into two teams. Draw a big tic-tac-toe board on the chalk board. Make one team X and one team O. Ask questions to each side, giving each student one turn. If the question is answered correctly, that student's team's letter (X or O) is placed in the box. If the answer is incorrect, no mark is placed in the box. The object is to get three marks in a row like tic-tac-toe. You may want to keep track of the number of games won for each team.

3. Take 1/2 period for students to make up true/false and short answer questions. Collect the questions. Divide the class into two teams. You'll alternate asking questions to individual members of teams A & B, like in a spelling bee. The question keeps going from A to B until it is correctly answered, then a new question is asked. A correct answer does not allow the team to get another question. Correct answers are +2 points; incorrect answers are -1 point.

4. Allow students time to quiz each other (in pairs) from their study guides and class notes.

5. Divide your class into two teams. Use the *There the Red Fern Grows* crossword words with their letters jumbled as a word list. Student 1 from Team A faces off against Student 1 from Team B. You write the first jumbled word on the board. The first student (1A or 1B) to unscramble the word wins the chance for his/her team to score points. If 1A wins the jumble, go to student 2A and give him/her a clue. He/she must give you the correct word which matches that clue. If he/she does, Team A scores a point, and you give student 3A a clue for which you expect another correct response. Continue giving Team A clues until some team member makes an incorrect response. An incorrect response sends the game back to the jumbled-word face off, this time with students 2A and 2B. Instead of repeating giving clues to the first few students of each team, continue with the student after the one who gave the last incorrect response on the team.

6. Take on the persona of "The Answer Person." Allow students to ask any question about the book. Answer the questions, or tell students where to look in the book to find the answer.

7. Students may enjoy playing charades with events from the story. Select a student to start. Give him/her a card with a scene or event from the story. Allow the players to use their books to find the scene being described. The first person to guess each charade performs the next one.

8. Play a categories-type quiz game. (A master is included in this Unit Plan.) Make an overhead transparency of the categories form. Divide the class into teams of three or four players each. Have each team choose a recorder and a banker. Choose a team to go first. That team will choose a category and point amount. Ask the question to the entire class. Use the Study Guide Quiz and Vocabulary questions. Give the teams one minute to discuss the answer and write it down. Walk around the room and check the answers. Each team that answers correctly receives the points. (Incorrect answers are not penalized; they just don't receive any points.) Cross out that square on the playing board. Play continues until all squares have been used. The winning team is the one with the most points. You can assign bonus points to any square or squares you choose.

9. Have students complete the last column (What I Learned) of the KWL sheet you distributed in Lesson One. Discuss their answers with the class.

NOTE: If students do not need the extra review, omit this lesson and go on to the test.

QUIZ GAME
Where the Red Fern Grows

Chapters I-IV	Chapters V-VII	Chapters VIII-IX	Chapters X-XII	Chapters XIII-XVI	Chapters XVII-XX
100	100	100	100	100	100
200	200	200	200	200	200
300	300	300	300	300	300
400	400	400	400	400	400
500	500	500	500	500	500

LESSON NINETEEN

Objective
    To test the students' understanding of the main ideas and themes in *Where the Red Fern Grows*

Activity #1
    Distribute the *Where the Red Fern Grows* Unit Tests. Go over the instructions in detail and allow the students the entire class period to complete the exam.

Activity #2
    Collect all test papers and assigned books prior to the end of the class period.

NOTES ABOUT THE UNIT TESTS IN THIS UNIT:

There are 5 different unit tests which follow.

There are two short answer tests which are based primarily on facts from the novel. The answer key for short answer unit test 1 follows the student test. The answer key for short answer test 2 follows the student short answer unit test 2.

There is one advanced short answer unit test. It is based on the extra discussion questions. Use the matching key for short answer unit test 2 to check the matching section of the advanced short answer unit test. There is no key for the short answer questions. The answers will be based on the discussions you have had during class.

There are two multiple choice unit tests. Following the two unit tests, you will find an answer sheet on which students should mark their answers. The same answer sheet should be used for both tests; however, students' answers will be different for each test. Following the students' answer sheet for the multiple choice tests you will find your answer keys.

The short answer tests have a vocabulary section. You should choose 20 of the vocabulary words from this unit, read them orally and have the students write them down. Then, either have students write a definition or use the words in sentences.

UNIT TESTS

SHORT ANSWER UNIT TEST 1 *Where the Red Fern Grows*

1. Matching/ Identify

_____ 1. Billy
_____ 2. Mama
_____ 3. Papa
_____ 4. Grandpa
_____ 5. Little Ann
_____ 6. Old Dan
_____ 7. mountain lion
_____ 8. coons
_____ 9. red fern
_____ 10. Rubin

A. prayed for a way to move to town
B. was afflicted with "puppy love"
C. smart, but gun-shy
D. sent away for the dogs
E. died while hunting the ghost coon
F. animal Billy and the dogs hunted
G. gave his son three steel traps
H. caused the death of the two dogs
I. strong and aggressive
J. subject of an Indian legend

II. Short Answers

1. Describe what Billy did to get his dogs. Include the things he did to earn the money, and his trip to pick the dogs up.

2. What did Billy say about his communication with his dogs?

3. Describe Billy's first coon hunt with his dogs.

Short Answer Unit Test 1 *Where the Red Fern Grows* continued

4. How did Mama, Papa, and Grandpa feel about Billy's hunting?

5. Describe one of Old Dan's or Little Ann's "predicaments" and how they got out of it.

6. Describe the evening Billy went hunting with the Pritchard boys. Include the reason they went hunting together, what they were hunting for, and what happened while they were hunting.

Short Answer Unit Test 1 *Where the Red Fern Grows* continued

7. Many of the dogs' actions at the hunting contest surprised the judge. Discuss the actions and why they surprised him.

8. Describe the events on the last night of the coon hunting contest.

9. Describe the fight between Old Dan and Little Ann and the mountain lion.

10. What did Billy discover the day the family left the Ozarks? What was the significance of the discovery?

Short Answer Unit Test 1 *Where the Red Fern Grows* continued

III. Essay

    Discuss Billy's growth and maturation from the beginning to the end of the novel. Include examples from the novel.

Short Answer Unit Test 1 *Where the Red Fern Grows*

IV. Vocabulary

Listen to the vocabulary words and spell them. After you have spelled all the words, go back and write down the definitions.

WORD	**DEFINITION**
1.	
2.	
3.	
4.	
5.	
6.	
7.	
8.	
9.	
10.	
11.	
12.	
13.	
14.	
15.	
16.	
17.	
18.	
19.	
20.	

ANSWER KEY SHORT ANSWER UNIT TEST 1 *Where the Red Fern Grows*

1. Matching/ Identify

B	1.	Billy	A.	prayed for a way to move to town
A	2.	Mama	B.	was afflicted with "puppy love"
G	3.	Papa	C.	smart, but gun-shy
D	4.	Grandpa	D.	sent away for the dogs
C	5.	Little Ann	E.	died while hunting the ghost coon
I	6.	Old Dan	F.	animal Billy and the dogs hunted
H	7.	mountain lion	G.	gave his son three steel traps
F	8.	coons	H.	caused the death of the two dogs
J	9.	red fern	I.	strong and aggressive
E	10.	Rubin	J.	subject of an Indian legend

II. Short Answers

1. Describe what Billy did to get his dogs. Include the things he did to earn the money, and his trip to pick the dogs up.

> He caught crawfish and other small fish and sold them to the fishermen for bait. He also sold them fresh vegetables and roasting corn. He picked blackberries and sold them to his grandfather. He used his traps in the winter and sold the furs to his grandfather. It took him two years to earn the fifty dollars he needed. He asked his grandfather to order the dogs. When they came in to the depot in Talequah, Billy walked the thirty miles to pick them up.

2. What did Billy say about his communication with his dogs?

> He said they could have heart-to-heart talks together. His dogs had a language of their own that was easy for him to understand. He could see answers in their eyes, in the way they wagged their tails, in their whines, and in the caress of their tongues.

3. Describe Billy's first coon hunt with his dogs.

> When Old Dan started bawling, Billy got a knot in his throat. Then he cried and whooped as the tears ran down his face. The hounds treed a raccoon in the largest sycamore tree on the bottoms. At first, Billy was discouraged because of the size of the tree. He told the dogs he was giving up. Then he looked at them and realized he couldn't disappoint them, so he vowed to cut the tree down. He chopped at the tree throughout the night. The next morning his grandfather made a scarecrow on the ground where the coon could see it, and Billy went home to eat and rest. Then he returned and kept chopping at the tree until his hands were so blistered that he couldn't chop any more. He was getting ready to go home when he heard the wind blowing in the top of the tree. The wind blew the tree over and the hounds caught the coon. Billy was sure the tree fell over because God was answering his prayer.

4. How did Mama, Papa, and Grandpa feel about Billy's hunting?

His father and grandfather supported him wholeheartedly. His grandfather encouraged him by giving advice and buying the skins. His father said he didn't need a lot of help on the farm and Billy could have the time to do his hunting. His mother was not happy about the idea, but agreed to let him go because he had worked so hard to get the dogs.

5. Describe one of Old Dan's or Little Ann's "predicaments" and how they got out of it.

Old Dan had followed a coon into an old muskrat den and was stuck. Billy dug him out and washed him off. Old Dan turned around and went back in after the coon. Billy and Little Ann helped dig the coon out and Old Dan killed him.

Another time Old Dan climbed up inside a hollow tree and out onto a branch to get a baby coon. Billy climbed up after him and pushed him back down the hole. Then he climbed down the tree. He caught Old Dan's tail as he was climbing back up the tree, and pulled him out. Then he blocked up the hole with rocks.

Little Ann chased a coon out onto the ice covered river and she fell through the ice into the river. Billy said a prayer to ask God to save her. Then he took the handle off his lantern, bent a hook onto one end, and tied it to the end of a cane pole. He took off his clothes and waded out into the icy river, breaking the ice with his axe as he went. He used the pole to get the hook under Little Ann's collar and dragged her out of the water. Once back on the bank, he made a fire and rubbed her to thaw her out. He attributed the rescue to God's help.

6. Describe the evening Billy went hunting with the Pritchard boys. Include the reason they went hunting together, what they were hunting for, and what happened while they were hunting.

Rubin wanted Billy to bet two dollars that his hounds could tree a certain old coon. When Billy refused, Rubin and Raine started taunting him. Billy's grandfather got angry and agreed to the bet. He put up the two dollars.

At one point while the boys were watching the dogs chase the coon, Billy said he felt good all over. He was happy because Rainie was whooping and screaming. Billy thought it was the first time in Rainie's life that he had been so excited.

Billy paid up on his bet because the dogs had not treed the coon. He was getting ready to leave when Little Ann caught the coon's scent when a breeze began stirring. It was hiding in a hollow gatepost. Billy decided he didn't want to kill the old coon because it had lived there such a long time.

Billy asked for his money back because his dogs had treed the coon. Rubin refused to give the money back. He threatened to knife Billy if he told his grandfather what had happened. Then he knocked Billy down and started whipping him in the face with his hat. Rainie joined in the fight. Meanwhile, the Pritchard boys' dog, Old Blue, had provoked a fight with Old Dan. Little Ann joined in and the two of them were killing Old Blue. Rubin grabbed Billy's axe and ran towards the dogs, intending to kill Old Dan and Little Ann. He tripped on a small stick and fell on the axe blade. Rainie saw him and ran away, screaming. Billy went to him and Rubin asked him to remove the axe. Billy did so, and Rubin died. Then Billy ran home and told his father what had happened.

7. Many of the dogs' actions at the hunting contest surprised the judge. Discuss the actions and why they surprised him.

> The judge was surprised that the dogs were able to find the scent when the coon had gone so far out on the river bottom. On the final night of the contest, he was surprised when the hounds stopped and stared at Billy before beginning to hunt. After the dogs had killed the coon, they licked and doctored each other's wounds. Finally, the judge was surprised that the hounds stayed with the treed coon through the sleet storm, even though they were covered with ice.

8. Describe the events on the last night of the coon hunting contest.

> There was a sleet storm. It was cold and icy. The judge said he thought they should all go back to camp, and leave the dogs where they were. Billy refused to leave his dogs. He said they would die before they would leave a coon in a tree. The three men finally agreed to stay with Billy and look for the dogs.
>
> Around five o'clock in the morning, Grandpa caught his foot in the fork of a broken elder limb. He was unconscious from the pain. Little Ann found him and Papa and the judge revived him. They carried him to a nearby gully and made him as comfortable as possible. Then they returned their attention to the dogs and the coon hunt. The dogs killed another coon.
>
> At daybreak they heard the other hunters whooping for them. Half of them took Grandpa back to camp to the doctor. The others went with Billy, his father, and the judge to find the dogs.
>
> The dogs were covered with ice and were walking in a circle around the treed coon. The men built a fire to thaw the dogs out. The dogs killed the coon, giving Billy his third skin of the night. When they returned to camp, The other hunters awarded Billy the cup and the money.

9. Describe the fight between Old Dan and Little Ann and the mountain lion.

> Billy and the dogs went to the Cyclone Timber country. Billy thought they had treed a bobcat. Then he saw Old Dan curl back his lips, snarl, and growl. Billy realized the dogs had treed a mountain lion. He was scared and called to Old Dan, but he would not leave.
>
> The mountain lion jumped from the tree. Old Dan met the mountain lion in mid air. Little Ann joined the fight. Billy joined in, fighting with his axe. When the lion charged at Billy, his dogs got between him and the lion. Billy returned to the fight and finally sank the blade into the lion's back. The lion died.
>
> As they were walking home, Billy discovered that Old Dan's belly had been slashed and his entrails were falling out. Billy pushed the entrails back into the wound and carried Old Dan home. Old Dan died soon after they arrived home. Billy buried him. A few days later Little Ann went to Old Dan's grave and died. The next day Billy buried her next to Old Dan.

10. What did Billy discover the day the family left the Ozarks? What was the significance of the discovery?

> He found a red fern growing between the two dogs' graves. According to an old Indian legend, any spot where the red fern grew was sacred.

III. Composition

Grade the compositions on your own criteria.

IV. Vocabulary

Choose an appropriate number of the vocabulary words to read orally for this section of the test.

SHORT ANSWER UNIT TEST 2 *Where the Red Fern Grows*

I. Matching/Identify

___ 1. Grandpa   A. was afflicted with "puppy love"
___ 2. mountain lion   B. gave his son three steel traps
___ 3. coons   C. prayed for a way to move to town
___ 4. Old Dan   D. caused the death of the two dogs
___ 5. Billy   E. sent away for the dogs
___ 6. Rubin   F. animal Billy and the dogs hunted
___ 7. Papa   G. subject of an Indian legend
___ 8. Little Ann   H. smart but gun-shy
___ 9. Mama   I. died while hunting the ghost coon
___ 10. red fern   J. strong and aggressive

II. Short Answer

1. What did Billy discover the day the family left the Ozarks? What was the significance of the discovery?

2. Describe what Billy did to get his dogs. Include the things he did to earn the money, and his trip to pick the dogs up.

3. Describe the fight between Old Dan and Little Ann and the mountain lion.

Short Answer Unit Test 2 Where *the Red Fern Grows* continued

4. How did Mama, Papa, and Grandpa feel about Billy's hunting?

5. Many of the dogs' actions at the hunting contest surprised the judge. Discuss the actions and why they surprised him.

6. Describe one of Old Dan's or Little Ann's "predicaments" and how they got out of it.

7. Describe the evening Billy went hunting with the Pritchard boys. Include the reason they went hunting together, what they were hunting for, and what happened while they were hunting.

Short Answer Unit Test 2 *Where the Red Fern Grows* continued

8. Describe the events on the last night of the coon hunting contest.

9. Describe Billy's first coon hunt with his dogs.

10. What did Billy say about his communication with his dogs?

Short Answer Unit Test 2 Where *the Red Fern Grows* continued

III. Essay

Identify the main themes in the novel and give specific examples to show each.

Short Answer Unit Test 2 Where *the Red Fern Grows* continued

IV. Vocabulary

Listen to the vocabulary words and spell them. After you have spelled all the words, go back and write down the definitions.

WORD	DEFINITION
1.	
2.	
3.	
4.	
5.	
6.	
7.	
8.	
9.	
10.	
11.	
12.	
13.	
14.	
15.	
16.	
17.	
18.	
19.	
20.	

ANSWER KEY SHORT ANSWER UNIT TEST 2 *Where the Red Fern Grows*

Use this key for the matching test for Short Answer Unit Test 2 and the Advanced Short Answer Test.

I. Matching/Identify

E	1.	Grandpa	A.	was afflicted with "puppy love"
D	2.	mountain lion	B.	gave his son three steel traps
F	3.	coons	C.	prayed for a way to move to town
J	4.	Old Dan	D.	caused the death of the two dogs
A	5.	Billy	E.	sent away for the dogs
I	6.	Rubin	F.	animal Billy and the dogs hunted
B	7.	Papa	G.	subject of an Indian legend
H	8.	Little Ann	H.	smart but gun-shy
C	9.	Mama	I.	died while hunting the ghost coon
G	10.	red fern	J.	strong and aggressive

II. Short Answer

1. What did Billy discover the day the family left the Ozarks? What was the significance of the discovery?

    He found a red fern growing between the two dogs' graves. According to an old Indian legend, any spot where the red fern grew was sacred.

2. Describe what Billy did to get his dogs. Include the things he did to earn the money, and his trip to pick the dogs up.

    He caught crawfish and other small fish and sold them to the fishermen for bait. He also sold them fresh vegetables and roasting corn. He picked blackberries and sold them to his grandfather. He used his traps in the winter and sold the furs to his grandfather. It took him two years to earn the fifty dollars he needed. He asked his grandfather to order the dogs. When they came in to the depot in Talequah, Billy walked the thirty miles to pick them up.

3. Describe the fight between Old Dan and Little Ann and the mountain lion.

    Billy and the dogs went to the Cyclone Timber country. Billy thought they had treed a bobcat. Then he saw Old Dan curl back his lips, snarl, and growl. Billy realized the dogs had treed a mountain lion. He was scared and called to Old Dan, but he would not leave. The mountain lion jumped from the tree. Old Dan met the mountain lion in mid air. Little Ann joined the fight. Billy joined in, fighting with his axe. When the lion charged at Billy, his dogs got between him and the lion. Billy returned to the fight and finally sank the blade into the lion's back. The lion died.

As they were walking home, Billy discovered that Old Dan's belly had been slashed and his entrails were falling out. Billy pushed the entrails back into the wound and carried Old Dan home. Old Dan died soon after they arrived home. Billy buried him. A few days later Little Ann went to Old Dan's grave and died. The next day Billy buried her next to Old Dan.

4. How did Mama, Papa, and Grandpa feel about Billy's hunting?
   His father and grandfather supported him wholeheartedly. His grandfather encouraged him by giving advice and buying the skins. His father said he didn't need a lot of help on the farm and Billy could have the time to do his hunting. His mother was not happy about the idea, but agreed to let him go because he had worked so hard to get the dogs.

5. Many of the dogs' actions at the hunting contest surprised the judge. Discuss the actions and why they surprised him.
   The judge was surprised that the dogs were able to ding the scent when the coon had gone so far out on the river bottom. On the final night of the contest, he was surprised when the hounds stopped and stared at Billy before beginning to hunt. After the dogs had killed the coon, they licked and doctored each other's wounds. Finally, the judge was surprised that the hounds stayed with the treed coon through the sleet storm, even though they were covered with ice.

6. Describe one of Old Dan's or Little Ann's "predicaments" and how they got out of it.
   Old Dan had followed a coon into an old muskrat den and was stuck. Billy dug him out and washed him off. Old Dan turned around and went back in after the coon. Billy and Little Ann helped dig the coon out and Old Dan killed him.
   Another time Old Dan climbed up inside a hollow tree and out onto a branch to get a baby coon. Billy climbed up after him and pushed him back down the hole. Then he climbed down the tree. He caught Old Dan's tail as he was climbing back up the tree and pulled him out. Then he blocked up the hole with rocks.
   Little Ann chased a coon out onto the ice covered river and she fell through the ice into the river. Billy said a prayer to ask God to save her. Then he took the handle off his lantern, bent a hook onto one end, and tied it to the end of a cane pole. He took off his clothes and waded out into the icy river, breaking the ice with his axe as he went. He used the pole to get the hook under Little Ann's collar and dragged her out of the water. Once back on the bank, he made a fire and rubbed her to thaw her out. He attributed the rescue to God's help.

7. Describe the evening Billy went hunting with the Pritchard boys. Include the reason they went hunting together, what they were hunting for, and what happened while they were hunting.

   Rubin wanted Billy to bet two dollars that his hounds could tree a certain old coon. When Billy refused, Rubin and Raine started taunting him. Billy's grandfather got angry and agreed to the bet. He put up the two dollars.

   At one point while the boys were watching the dogs chase the coon, Billy said he felt good all over. He was happy because Rainie was whooping and screaming. Billy thought it was the first time in Rainie's life that he had been so excited.

   Billy paid up on his bet because the dogs had not treed the coon. He was getting ready to leave when Little Ann caught the coon's scent when a breeze began stirring. It was hiding in a hollow gatepost. Billy decided he didn't want to kill the old coon because it had lived there such a long time.

   Billy asked for his money back because his dogs had treed the coon. Rubin refused to give the money back. He threatened to knife Billy if he told his grandfather what had happened. Then he knocked Billy down and started whipping him in the face with his hat. Rainie joined in the fight. Meanwhile, the Pritchard boys' dog, Old Blue, had provoked a fight with Old Dan. Little Ann joined in and the two of them were killing Old Blue. Rubin grabbed Billy's axe and ran towards the dogs, intending to kill Old Dan and Little Ann. He tripped on a small stick and fell on the axe blade. Rainie saw him and ran away, screaming. Billy went to him and Rubin asked him to remove the axe. Billy did so, and Rubin died. Then Billy ran home and told his father what had happened.

8. Describe the events on the last night of the coon hunting contest.

   There was a sleet storm. It was cold and icy. The judge said he thought they should all go back to camp, and leave the dogs where they were. Billy refused to leave his dogs. He said they would die before they would leave a coon in a tree. The three men finally agreed to stay with Billy and look for the dogs.

   Around five o'clock in the morning, Grandpa caught his foot in the fork of a broken elder limb. He was unconscious from the pain. Little Ann found him and Papa and the judge revived him. They carried him to a nearby gully and made him as comfortable as possible. Then they returned their attention to the dogs and the coon hunt. The dogs killed another coon.

   At daybreak they heard the other hunters whooping for them. Half of them took Grandpa back to camp to the doctor. The others went with Billy, his father, and the judge to find the dogs.

   The dogs were covered with ice and were walking in a circle around the treed coon. The men built a fire to thaw the dogs out. The dogs killed the coon, giving Billy his third skin of the night.

   When they returned to camp, The other hunters awarded Billy the cup and the money.

9. Describe Billy's first coon hunt with his dogs.
   When Old Dan started bawling, Billy got a knot in his throat. Then he cried and whooped as the tears ran down his face. The hounds treed a raccoon in the largest sycamore tree on the bottoms. At first, Billy was discouraged because of the size of the tree. He told the dogs he was giving up. Then he looked at them and realized he couldn't disappoint them, so he vowed to cut the tree down. He chopped at the tree throughout the night. The next morning his grandfather made a scarecrow on the ground where the coon could see it, and Billy went home to eat and rest. Then he returned and kept chopping at the tree until his hands were so blistered that he couldn't chop any more. He was getting ready to go home when he heard the wind blowing in the top of the tree. The wind blew the tree over and the hounds caught the coon. Billy was sure the tree fell over because God was answering his prayer.

10. What did Billy say about his communication with his dogs?
    He said they could have heart-to-heart talks together. His dogs had a language of their own that was easy for him to understand. He could see answers in their eyes, in the way they wagged their tails, in their whines, and in the caress of their tongues.

III. Composition Grade the composition on your own criteria.

IV. Vocabulary Choose an appropriate number of vocabulary words to read orally for this section of the test.

ADVANCED SHORT ANSWER TEST *Where the Red Fern Grows*

I. Matching/Identify

____ 1. Grandpa   A. was afflicted with "puppy love"
____ 2. mountain lion   B. gave his son three steel traps
____ 3. coons   C. prayed for a way to move to town
____ 4. Old Dan   D. caused the death of the two dogs
____ 5. Billy   E. sent away for the dogs
____ 6. Rubin   F. animal Billy and the dogs hunted
____ 7. Papa   G. subject of an Indian legend
____ 8. Little Ann   H. smart but gun-shy
____ 9. Mama   I. died while hunting the ghost coon
____ 10. red fern   J. strong and aggressive

II. Short Answer

1. Identify the main themes in the novel and give examples of each.

2. Discuss Billy's growth and maturation from the ages of ten through fourteen.

Advanced Short Answer Test *Where the Red Fern Grows*

3. Discuss the role of religion in the novel.

4. Early in the novel, the narrator describes Old Dan as being the aggressive one and Little Ann as being the smart one. Give examples of the way that the writer shows this to be true.

5. Was the dogs' death important to the novel? Why or why not?

Advanced Short Answer Test *Where the Red Fern Grows*

III. Quotations
  Explain the importance and meaning of the following quotations.

1. "It's all over," I said. "There'll be no more sessions. I've worked hard and I've done my best. From now on it's all up to you. Hunting season is just a few days away and I'm going to let you rest for I want you to be in good shape the night it opens."

2. "Men," said Mr. Kyle, "people have been trying to understand dogs ever since the beginning of time. One never knows what they'll do. You can read every day where a dog saved the life of a drowning child, or lay down his life for his master. Some people call this loyalty. I don't. I may be wrong, but I call it love-the deepest kind of love."

3. "It's a shame that people all over the world can't have that kind of love in their hearts," he said. "There would be no wars, slaughter, or murder; no greed or selfishness. It would be the kind of world that God wants us to have--a wonderful world."

Advanced Short Answer Test *Where the Red Fern Grows*

4. "Billy," he said, "there are times in a boy's life when he has to stand up like a man. This is one of those times. I know what you're going through and how it hurts, but there's always an answer. The Good Lord has a reason for everything He does."

5. I heard him mutter, "There's not a one in that bunch with that kind of grit."

Advanced Short Answer Test *Where the Red Fern Grows*

IV. Vocabulary

    Listen to the words and write them down. After you have written down all of the words, write a paragraph in which you use all the words. The paragraph must in some way relate to *Where the Red Fern Grows*.

MULTIPLE CHOICE UNIT TEST 1 *Where the Red Fern Grows*

1. Matching/ Identify

____ 1. Billy	A.	prayed for a way to move to town
____ 2. Mama	B.	was afflicted with "puppy love"
____ 3. Papa	C.	smart, but gun-shy
____ 4. Grandpa	D.	sent away for the dogs
____ 5. Little Ann	E.	died while hunting the ghost coon
____ 6. Old Dan	F.	animal Billy and the dogs hunted
____ 7. mountain lion	G.	gave his son three steel traps
____ 8. coons	H.	caused the death of the two dogs
____ 9. red fern	I.	strong and aggressive
____ 10. Rubin	J.	subject of an Indian legend

II. Multiple Choice

1. How did the boy earn the money to get what he wanted?
      A. He worked in other men's fields. He grew vegetables and sold them to tourists. He picked blackberries and sold them to his grandfather. He trapped small animals and sold the furs to his grandfather.
      B. He sold bait, fresh vegetables, and roasting corn to the fishermen. He picked blackberries and sold them to his grandfather. His grandfather paid him to deliver items from the store to the customers.
      C. He cleaned and skinned fish for the fishermen, planted and maintained gardens for the neighboring women, and did odd jobs around his grandfather's store.
      D. He sold bait, fresh vegetables, and roasting corn to the fishermen. He picked blackberries and sold them to his grandfather. He trapped small animals and sold the furs to his grandfather.

2. What did Billy say about his communication with his dogs?
      A. He said they could have heart-to-heart talks together. His dogs had a language of their own that was easy for him to understand.
      B. He said they were dumb animals who needed to be trained to take orders.
      C. He said Little Ann was able to communicate, but Old Dan wasn't because he was deaf.
      D. He said Little Ann would only communicate with his sisters, and Old Dan would only communicate with him.

Multiple Choice Unit Test 1 *Where the Red Fern Grows*

3. How did Billy's parents feel about his hunting?
    A. They both approved wholeheartedly. They said it was the way of the mountain folk and they were proud of him for carrying on the tradition.
    B. His mother strongly disapproved and wanted him to stop. His father told his mother that he was the head of the family and would make the decision. He said it was fine.
    C. His parents both disapproved but his grandfather convinced them to let him try it. He said Billy would get bored after a week or so and stop hunting.
    D. His mother was worried but felt she could not stop him because of all he had done to get the dogs. His father thought it was fine because he was getting to be a man.

4. What did Billy decide to do about the coon the dogs treed in the big sycamore?
    A. He was satisfied that they treed the coon. He said he didn't need to kill it to prove they were competent hunters.
    B. He said he would help his dogs get the coon out of the tree no matter what it took.
    C. He set traps around the bottom of the tree so the coon would get caught if it tried to climb down.
    D. He decided to let his father and grandfather catch the coon since they had more experience than he did.

5. What were Old Dan's predicaments, and how were they resolved ?
    A. Old Dan climbed a tree and couldn't get down. Billy climbed a ladder to bring him down. He also got his paw stuck in a steel trap and Billy pried it loose.
    B. Old Dan got too close to a skunk and was sprayed. Billy gave him a bath every day for two weeks to get the smell out. He also got stuck in a beaver den, and Billy and Little Ann dug him out.
    C. Old Dan fell into a patch of poison ivy. Billy petted him and they both had poison ivy for several weeks. He also tried to jump a barbed wire fence and got cut up.
    D. Old Dan got stuck in an old muskrat den, and Billy and Little Ann dug him out. He also climbed up inside a hollow tree and out onto a branch. Billy climbed up after him and pushed him back down the hole.

Multiple Choice Unit Test 1 *Where the Red Fern Grows*

6. How did Billy rescue Little Ann when she fell through the ice into the river?
    A. He put a piece of meat on a long pole and stretched it out to Little Ann. When she bit on the meat he pulled on the pole and dragged her in.
    B. He made a hook from his lantern handle and tied it to a pole. He waded out into the river, got the hook under her collar, and dragged her out of the water.
    C. The water was only waist deep on him. He waded out, breaking the ice with his axe. He put Little Ann under one arm and waded back to shore with her.
    D. He tied a rope around his waist and around a tree. He walked out as far as he could. Then he used another rope to lasso Little Ann and pull her out.

7. What happened to Rubin while the boys were hunting the ghost coon?
    A. The coon bit him and he later died of rabies.
    B. He tripped on a small stick, fell on the axe blade, and died.
    C. He accidentally killed his dog during the fight.
    D. He fell into the river and drowned. Billy didn't know Rubin could not swim.

8. After the dogs killed the coon, what did they do that surprised the judge?
    A. He was surprised when the dogs went off alone to clean their wounds.
    B. He was surprised when the dogs started fighting each other.
    C. He was surprised when the dogs started licking and doctoring each other's wounds.
    D. He was surprised when the dogs tore the coon apart.

9. What happened to the dogs during the last night of the hunting contest?
    A. They had a severe case of frostbite and had to be taken back to camp.
    B. They fell asleep under the tree and the raccoon escaped.
    C. They killed the coon after the men thawed them out.
    D. They lost the coon's scent because of the heavy sleet.

10. According to an old Indian legend, what was the significance of the red fern?
    A. Any spot where the red fern grew was sacred.
    B. The fern grew on a spot where blood had been shed.
    C. The first person to see it would never return to that spot again.
    D. Whoever lived on the land where the fern grew would have good luck in life.

Multiple Choice Unit Test 1 *Where the Red Fern Grows*

III. Quotations

Identify the speaker.
A. Billy B. the marshal C. Papa D. Mama
E. Grandpa F. Mr. Kyle G. a hunter

1. "Well, son, it's your money. You worked for it, and you worked hard. You got it honestly, and you want some dogs. We're going to get those dogs. Be darned! Be darned!"

2. "There's not a one in that bunch with that kind of grit."

3. "I don't want you to feel badly about the people in town. I don't think they were poking fun at you, anyway not like you think they were."

4. "It's all over. There'll be no more sessions. I've worked hard and I've done my best. From now on it's all up to you. Hunting season is just a few days away and I'm going to let you rest for I want you to be in good shape the night it opens."

5. " I don't approve of this hunting but it looks like I can't say no; not after all you've been through, getting your dogs, and all that training."

6. "Men, people have been trying to understand dogs ever since the beginning of time. One never knows what they'll do. You can read every day where a dog saved the life of a drowning child, or lay down his life for his master. Some people call this loyalty. I don't. I may be wrong, but I call it love-the deepest kind of love."

7. "It's a shame that people all over the world can't have that kind of love in their hearts. There would be no wars, slaughter, or murder; no greed or selfishness. It would be the kind of world that God wants us to have--a wonderful world."

8. "You were worth it, old friend, and a thousand times over."

9. "You've done no wrong, Billy. I know it hurts, but at one time or another, everyone suffers. Even the Good Lord suffered while He was here on earth."

10. "There are times in a boy's life when he has to stand up like a man. This is one of those times. I know what you're going through and how it hurts, but there's always an answer. The Good Lord has a reason for everything He does."

Multiple Choice Unit Test 1 *Where the Red Fern Grows*

IV. Vocabulary

1.	astonished	A.	boldly resisting
2.	belligerent	B.	cunning
3.	cleaved	C.	living by hunting other organisms
4.	commotion	D.	filled with wonder or amazement
5.	defiant	E.	having a fine, sharp blade
6.	dormant	F.	sudden sharp spasms of pain
7.	drastic	G.	the point beyond which an action is likely to begin
8.	eerie	H.	severe or radical in nature
9.	gloated	I.	a sudden forward movement or plunge
10.	keen	J.	inclined or eager to fight; hostile or aggressive
11.	lunge	K.	to satisfy
12.	nonchalantly	L.	expressed great, often malicious self-satisfaction
13.	notion	M.	serious, grave, or solemn
14.	obstacle	N.	an agitated disturbance
15.	pangs	O.	one that opposes or stands in the way of progress
16.	predatory	P.	strange and frightening
17.	quench	Q.	unconcernedly or indifferently
18.	sober	R.	pierced or penetrated
19.	verge	S.	a mental image or idea
20.	wiley	T.	latent but capable of being activated

Multiple Choice Unit Test 2 *Where the Red Fern Grows*

I. Matching/ Identify

___ 1.	Grandpa	A.	was afflicted with "puppy love"
___ 2.	mountain lion	B.	gave his son three steel traps
___ 3.	coons	C.	prayed for a way to move to town
___ 4.	Old Dan	D.	caused the death of the two dogs
___ 5.	Billy	E.	sent away for the dogs
___ 6.	Rubin	F.	animal Billy and the dogs hunted
___ 7.	Papa	G.	subject of an Indian legend
___ 8.	Little Ann	H.	smart but gun-shy
___ 9.	Mama	I.	died while hunting the ghost coon
___ 10.	red fern	J.	strong and aggressive

II. Multiple Choice

1. How did Billy's parents feel about his hunting?
    A. They both approved wholeheartedly. They said it was the way of the mountain folk and they were proud of him for carrying on the tradition.
    B. His mother strongly disapproved and wanted him to stop. His father told his mother that he was the head of the family and would make the decision. He said it was fine.
    C. His parents both disapproved but his grandfather convinced them to let him try it. He said Billy would get bored after a week or so and stop hunting.
    D. His mother was worried but felt she could not stop him because of all he had done to get the dogs. His father thought it was fine because he was getting to be a man.

2. What were Old Dan's predicaments, and how were they resolved?
    A. Old Dan climbed a tree and couldn't get down. Billy climbed a ladder to bring him down. He also got his paw stuck in a steel trap and Billy pried it loose.
    B. Old Dan got too close to a skunk and was sprayed. Billy gave him a bath every day for two weeks to get the smell out. He also got stuck in a beaver den, and Billy and Little Ann dug him out.
    C. Old Dan fell into a patch of poison ivy. Billy petted him and they both had poison ivy for several weeks. He also tried to jump a barbed wire fence and got cut up.
    D. Old Dan got stuck in an old muskrat den, and Billy and Little Ann dug him out. He also climbed up inside a hollow tree and out onto a branch. Billy climbed up after him and pushed him back down the hole.

Multiple Choice Unit Test 2 *Where the Red Fern Grows*

3. After the dogs killed the coon, what did they do that surprised the judge?
    A. He was surprised when the dogs went off alone to clean their wounds.
    B. He was surprised when the dogs started fighting each other.
    C. He was surprised when the dogs started licking and doctoring each other's wounds.
    D. He was surprised when the dogs tore the coon apart.

4. According to an old Indian legend, what was the significance of the red fern?
    A. Any spot where the red fern grew was sacred.
    B. The fern grew on a spot where blood had been shed.
    C. The first person to see it would never return to that spot again.
    D. Whoever lived on the land where the fern grew would have good luck in life.

5. What happened to Rubin while the boys were hunting the ghost coon?
    A. The coon bit him and he later died of rabies.
    B. He tripped on a small stick, fell on the axe blade, and died.
    C. He accidentally killed his dog during the fight.
    D. He fell into the river and drowned. Billy didn't know Rubin could not swim.

6. What did Billy decide to do about the coon the dogs treed in the big sycamore?
    A. He was satisfied that they treed the coon. He said he didn't need to kill it to prove they were competent hunters.
    B. He said he would help his dogs get the coon out of the tree no matter what it took.
    C. He set traps around the bottom of the tree so the coon would get caught if it tried to climb down.
    D. He decided to let his father and grandfather catch the coon since they had more experience than he did.

Multiple Choice Unit Test 2 *Where the Red Fern Grows*

7. How did the boy earn the money to get what he wanted?
    A. He worked in other men's fields. He grew vegetables and sold them to tourists. He picked blackberries and sold them to his grandfather. He trapped small animals and sold the furs to his grandfather.
    B. He sold bait, fresh vegetables, and roasting corn to the fishermen. He picked blackberries and sold them to his grandfather. His grandfather paid him to deliver items from the store to the customers.
    C. He cleaned and skinned fish for the fishermen, planted and maintained gardens for the neighboring women, and did odd jobs around his grandfather's store.
    D. He sold bait, fresh vegetables, and roasting corn to the fishermen. He picked blackberries and sold them to his grandfather. He trapped small animals and sold the furs to his grandfather.

8. How did Billy rescue Little Ann when she fell through the ice into the river?
    A. He put a piece of meat on a long pole and stretched it out to Little Ann. When she bit on the meat he pulled on the pole and dragged her in.
    B. He made a hook from his lantern handle and tied it to a pole. He waded out into the river, got the hook under her collar, and dragged her out of the water.
    C. The water was only waist deep on him. He waded out, breaking the ice with his axe. He put Little Ann under one arm and waded back to shore with her.
    D. He tied a rope around his waist and around a tree. He walked out as far as he could. Then he used another rope to lasso Little Ann and pull her out.

9. What did Billy say about his communication with his dogs?
    A. He said they could have heart-to-heart talks together. His dogs had a language of their own that was easy for him to understand.
    B. He said they were dumb animals who needed to be trained to take orders.
    C. He said Little Ann was able to communicate, but Old Dan wasn't because he was deaf.
    D. He said Little Ann would only communicate with his sisters, and Old Dan would only communicate with him.

10. What happened to the dogs during the last night of the hunting contest?
    A. They had a severe case of frostbite and had to be taken back to camp.
    B. They fell asleep under the tree and the coon escaped.
    C. They killed the coon after the men thawed them out.
    D. They lost the coon's scent because of the heavy sleet.

Multiple Choice Unit Test 2 *Where the Red Fern Grows*

III. Quotations   Identify the speaker.
   A. Billy   B. the marshal   C. Papa   D. Mama
E   . Grandpa   F. Mr. Kyle   G. a hunter

1. "It's all over. There'll be no more sessions. I've worked hard and I've done my best. From now on it's all up to you. Hunting season is just a few days away and I'm going to let you rest for I want you to be in good shape the night it opens."

2. "You were worth it, old friend, and a thousand times over."

3. "Well, son, it's your money. You worked for it, and you worked hard. You got it honestly, and you want some dogs. We're going to get those dogs. Be darned! Be darned!"

4. "There are times in a boy's life when he has to stand up like a man. This is one of those times. I know what you're going through and how it hurts, but there's always an answer. The Good Lord has a reason for everything He does."

5. "Men, people have been trying to understand dogs ever since the beginning of time. One never knows what they'll do. You can read every day where a dog saved the life of a drowning child, or lay down his life for his master. Some people call this loyalty. I don't. I may be wrong, but I call it love-the deepest kind of love."

6. "There's not a one in that bunch with that kind of grit."

7. "You've done no wrong, Billy. I know it hurts, but at one time or another, everyone suffers. Even the Good Lord suffered while He was here on earth."

8. "I don't want you to feel badly about the people in town. I don't think they were poking fun at you, anyway not like you think they were."

9. " I don't approve of this hunting but it looks like I can't say no; not after all you've been through, getting your dogs, and all that training."

10. "It's a shame that people all over the world can't have that kind of love in their hearts. There would be no wars, slaughter, or murder; no greed or selfishness. It would be the kind of world that God wants us to have--a wonderful world."

Multiple Choice Unit Test 2 *Where the Red Fern Grows*

IV. Vocabulary Matching

1. begrudgingly
2. berserk
3. caress
4. coaxing
5. convenient
6. dazed
7. domain
8. doused
9. gingerly
10. hampering
11. limber
12. lull
13. mulled
14. notched
15. pace
16. peculiarity
17. predicament
18. probed
19. squabble
20. vicious

A. the rate of speed at which a person walks or runs
B. destructively or frenetically violent
C. preventing the free movement or progress of
D. a territory over which rule or control is exercised
E. explored; investigated
F. marked by an aggressive disposition; savage
G. put out; extinguished
H. reluctantly
I. a gentle touch or gesture of fondness
J. bending or flexible
K. a noisy quarrel
L. with great care or delicacy; cautiously
M. an unpleasant or troublesome situation
N. persuading by pleading or flattery
O. a relatively calm interval
P. a notable or distinctive feature or characteristic
Q. easy to reach; accessible
R. gone over extensively in the mind
S. stunned; stupefied
T. made a V-shaped cut in

ANSWER SHEET MULTIPLE CHOICE UNIT TESTS - *Where the Red Fern Grows*

	I. Matching	II. Multiple Choice	III. Quotations	IV. Vocabulary
1				
2				
3				
4				
5				
6				
7				
8				
9				
10				
11				
12				
13				
14				
15				
16				
17				
18				
19				
20				

ANSWER KEY MULTIPLE CHOICE UNIT TEST 1 - *Where the Red Fern Grows*

	I. Matching	II. Multiple Choice	III. Quotations	IV. Vocabulary
1	B	D	E	D
2	A	A	B	J
3	G	D	C	R
4	D	B	A	N
5	C	D	D	A
6	I	B	F	T
7	H	B	G	H
8	F	C	A	P
9	J	C	D	L
10	E	A	C	E
11				I
12				Q
13				S
14				O
15				F
16				C
17				K
18				M
19				G
20				B

ANSWER KEY MULTIPLE CHOICE UNIT TEST 2 - *Where the Red Fern Grows*

	I. Matching	II. Multiple Choice	III. Quotations	IV. Vocabulary
1	E	D	A	H
2	D	D	A	B
3	F	C	E	I
4	J	A	C	N
5	A	B	F	Q
6	I	B	B	S
7	B	D	D	D
8	H	B	C	G
9	C	A	D	L
10	G	C	G	C
11				J
12				O
13				R
14				T
15				A
16				P
17				M
18				E
19				K
20				F

UNIT RESOURCE MATERIALS

BULLETIN BOARD IDEAS *Where the Red Fern Grows*

1. Save one corner of the board for the best of students' *Where the Red Fern Grows* writing assignments. You may want to use background maps of Oklahoma and the Ozark mountain area to represent the setting of the novel.

2. Take one of the word search puzzles from the extra activities packet and with a marker copy it over in a large size on the bulletin board. Write the clue words to find to one side. Invite students prior to and after class to find the words and circle them on the bulletin board.

3. Have students find or draw pictures that they think resemble the people and animals in the book.

4. Invite students to help make an interactive bulletin board quiz. Give each student a half-sheet of paper (about 4"x5') folded in half so that it can open. On the outside flap, have each student write a description of one of the characters in the text. On the inside, they will write the name of the character. You can staple or tack these papers to the bulletin board so that the students can read the descriptions and lift the flaps to find the answers.

5. Collect pictures of the localities mentioned in the book.

6. Make a display of travel posters of Oklahoma, Kentucky, and the whole Ozark Mountain area.

7. Have students design postcards depicting the settings of the book.

8. Have students design tombstones for the dogs. Write epitaphs on them.

9. Collect pictures of different breeds of dogs and display them. Write a 2-4 sentence summary about each dog.

10. Invite students to display pictures of themselves with their pets.

11. Design and display prize ribbons, cups, medals, etc.

12. Make a display of classified advertisements for pets.

EXTRA ACTIVITIES *Where the Red Fern Grows*

One of the difficulties in teaching a novel is that all students don't read at the same speed. One student who likes to read may take the book home and finish it in a day or two. Sometimes a few students finish the in-class assignments early. The problem, then, is finding suitable extra activities for students.

One thing that helps is to keep a little library in the classroom. For this unit on *Where the Red Fern Grows* you might check out from the school or public library *The Summer of the Monkeys,* another book by Wilson Rawls. There are also many other novels about people and their pets that students would enjoy reading.

The novel is available on audio tape. Your students who have reading difficulties, or speak English as a second language may benefit from listening to all or part of the book on tape.

Other things you may keep on hand are word search puzzles. Several puzzles relating directly to *Where the Red Fern Grows* are included in the unit. Feel free to duplicate them.

Some students may like to draw. You might devise a contest or allow some extra-credit grade for students who draw characters or scenes from *Where the Red Fern Grows.* Note, too, that if the students do not want to keep their drawings you may pick up some extra bulletin board materials this way. If you have a contest and you supply the prize. You could, possibly, make the drawing itself a non-refundable entry fee.

The pages which follow contain games, puzzles, and worksheets. The keys, when appropriate, immediately follow the puzzle or worksheet. There are two main groups of activities: one group for the unit; that is, generally relating to the *Where the Red Fern Grows* text, and another group of activities related strictly to the *Where the Red Fern Grows* vocabulary.

Directions for the games, puzzles, and worksheets are self-explanatory. The object here is to provide you with extra materials you may use in any way you choose.

MORE ACTIVITIES *Where the Red Fern Grows*

1. Pick one of the incidents for students to dramatize. Encourage students to write dialog for the characters. (Perhaps you could assign various stories to different groups of students so more than one story could be acted and more students could participate.)

2. Have students design a book cover (front and back and inside flaps) for *Where the Red Fern Grows.*

3. Have students design a bulletin board (ready to be put up; not just sketched) for *Where the Red Fern Grows.*

4. Invite a story teller to tell one or more stories related to *Where the Red Fern Grows* to the class.

5. Use some of the related topics (noted earlier for an in-class library) as topics for research, reports, written papers, or as topics for guest speakers.

6. Help students design and produce a talk show. Choose one of the story incidents as the topic. The host will interview the various characters. (Students should make up the questions they want the host to ask the characters.)

7. Have students work in pairs to create an interview with one of the characters. One student should be the interviewer and the other should be the interviewee. Students can work together to compose questions for the interviewer to ask. Each pair of students could present their interview to the class.

8. Invite students who have read the another by Wilson Rawls, or similar books, to present book talks to the class.

9. Invite someone who has lived in one of the areas mentioned in the book to speak to the class.

10. Have students hold small group discussions related to topics in the book. Assign a recorder and a speaker for each group. Have the speaker from each group make a report to the class.

11. Invite a member of a local hunting association to give their viewpoint about hunting as a sport. Prepare questions ahead of time to ask the person.

12. Invite a member of the local SPCA or other animal rights group to give their viewpoint about hunting as a sport. Prepare questions ahead of time to ask the person.

13. Have a class debate on the pros and cons of hunting for sport. Use the information from the two speakers to support the opposing points of view.

14. Re-write a portion of the story from Little Ann's or Old Dan's point of view.

15. Write a eulogy for the dogs.

16. Make dioramas to depict a scene from the book.

17. Read other Indian legends like the one of the red fern and summarize them for the class.

18. Read more about hunting dogs. Give a short report to the class.

19. Have students who have lived in the city and students who have lived in rural areas compare and contrast the different life styles.

20. Develop a plan for moving from one area to another. Make a schedule or a time line for all of the activities that are involved in a move (selling the current house, buying a new house, finding a new job, hiring movers, etc.) Estimate costs for the move.

21. Write another chapter of the book about Billy's new life in town.

23. Write a *Where the Red Fern Grows* newspaper. Divide students into groups. Have each group write a news article based on one section of the book. Put the articles together into a newspaper. Give the paper an appropriate title.

24. Invite groups of students to dramatize favorite portions of the story.

25. Play a picture identification game. Have individual students draw pictures of scenes from the book. Have other students tell what the scene is. Encourage them to re-read the text to find the exact portion of the novel. The student who correctly identifies the picture has the option of keeping it.

UNIT WORD SEARCH *Where the Red Fern Grows*

All the words in this list are associated with *Where the Red Fern Grows* with emphasis on the characters and events. The words are placed backwards, forward, diagonally up and down. The clues below the word search will help identify the words.

```
P R I T C H A R D N M N F S Y O V O K K N Z Q N N A E L T T I S L H I
F L O W E R S K O D T R A R M V K W J M Q N M T I D M B Y J O T L X L
S O W Z C V W I V Z B M R O K F I C O M P F R O Z E C M P L E W C B I
Q T M F M L T R T E I A S I Z I N L O G A T E P O S T P D T W O S S M
U R O M L C T K J E M E A G N G M U D W K O L E R C A D Q S U D U X B
B Q I R E K B A V H J P H V C G N D A V G G V D L A A Z G E L O P N P
X G B L E M L R Q B L Y H P K T T L P Z Q R J P Y N M H K T I L X S T
Z J F F U G U B W S L L Q M A Z J A M Q Y A P A D O I H B N M L Z I F
D E V C N H B V C W B R S I K T L O I Q B N I C V Z X O T O J A C G Z
R F O S O Y Z R P P M I N W N P V S L L F D A N Y A N W M C Z R U Z T
Z V T E T A Q R T Y C L L W G P X N Z D L P B I U R S S H M X S M J S
C O O N H U N T P Q I J I L K H U D K F B A L H X K L A U O I Y G I K
I S T V P W H E Q O S Q A E Y G O G P A N L H C P S U M D K O F N N L
G Z V P E B S W N D K R E Z Y J C S O L I K U S K Z S H Q B N P J M G
S S C I N V S L E E T K A B D D N I T N T Z H E R O N K A U U F R F S
B I D O Q N G P N X O G X Y V E U J O C H T N B S A L Q G P V E O U P
G J V S K J G A K R B O H J J Y D I N D O R N V C W M G N W N U K O Y
Z H X I C L V D E Z C K Z D T C S H V F E O S C D N B F Q E L F E Y K
A D H A R W Q H B Z G Y T F U U B O J F G T N N U Q O L U G B C Y M G
V P E V L X C S G F V G M Z M A M A D N A L G N E W E N B D L F L L E
O Y A S M Q P Q N U O D B W I Q X E S O F M F A L Q J T S U Y H H H C
N X J P M P I H S Y F N G T J U R W C M P Y V P Z N B E V J N D A L M
```

BILLY	DEPOT	COATS
MAMA	FLOWERS	NEW ENGLAND
PAPA	RED FERN	SLEET
GRANDPA	JUDGE	GATE POST
LITTLE ANN	CONTEST	STORE
OLD DAN	MARSHAL	COON HUNT
PRITCHARD	REFLECTION	SAMIE
OLD BLUE	GUN	ILLINOIS
OZARKS	WHOOP	CHEROKEE
GHOST COON	MR RINGTAIL	TWO DOLLARS
MOUNTAIN LION	CAP	

CROSSWORD *Where the Red Fern Grows*

CROSSWORD CLUES *Where the Red Fern Grows*

ACROSS
1 Where the coon hid: gate ___
3 Location of the big sycamore tree
5 Curious cat
7 Grandpa entered the hounds in one
10 Rescued Billy from the fight with the town children
14 Attacked Billy and the dogs: mountain ___
15 The Pritchard's hound: Old ___
16 Fell on the axe and died
20 Grew on a sacred spot: red ___
22 Billy carried the puppies home in one: gunny ___
23 Strong and aggressive: Old ___
25 Was amazed at Billy's dogs
26 Where Grandpa worked
28 Cup Billy gave to his youngest sister
31 Dollar cost of the hounds
33 Dollar amount Billy spent on gifts for the family
34 Gave Billy three steel traps
35 Fad for coon skin ones raised the price of skins
37 Was afflicted with "puppy love"
38 Mama's Indian heritage
39 Rubin and Rainie's last name

DOWN
2 Dollar amount of Grandpa's bet with the Pritchard boys
3 Grandpa made one with the Pritchard boys
4 Prayed for a way to move to town
5 Cup Little Ann won at the beauty contest
6 Sound Billy made to the hounds
7 Billy didn't want to kill it: ghost ___
8 Where coonskin coat fad was: New ___
9 Number of Billy's sisters
11 Author
12 River near the bottoms
13 Billy's other desire
17 Billy used a K.C. ___ Powder can for a bank
18 Billy saw his for the first time on his trip to town
19 Sent away for the dogs
21 Thought about and talked to frequently by Billy
22 Weather during last night of the coon hunting contest
24 Smart but gun-shy: Little ___
27 Town Billy walked to for the dogs
29 Mountain setting of the novel
30 Was excited on the hunt for the ghost coon
31 Dollar amount Billy saved
32 Nickname for a raccoon: Mr. ___
36 Billy thought the hounds had treed one
38 Mama made one from Billy's first coon skin

CROSSWORD ANSWER KEY *Where the Red Fern Grows*

MATCHING QUIZ 1 *Where the Red Fern Grows*

____	1. bet	A.	mountain setting of novel
____	2. bobcat	B.	was amazed by Billy's dogs
____	3. Cherokee	C.	Grandpa entered the hounds in one
____	4. contest	D.	last name of Rubin and Rainie
____	5. fifty	E.	dollar amount Billy saved
____	6. forty	F.	Billy carried the puppies in one
____	7. ghost coon	G.	Billy thought he heard one while hunting
____	8. God	H.	prayed for a way to move to town
____	9. Grandpa	I.	Billy didn't want to kill it
____	10. gunny sack	J.	town where Billy picked up his puppies
____	11. judge	K.	the scourge of the mountains
____	12. Kentucky	L.	Grandpa made one with Pritchard boys
____	13. Mama	M.	thought about and talked to frequently by Billy
____	14. mountain lion	N.	Pritchards' hound
____	15. New England	O.	Mama's Indian heritage
____	16. Old Blue	P.	Billy's strongest supporter
____	17. Ozarks	Q.	location of coonskin coat fad
____	18. Pritchard	R.	dollar amount Billy spent on the hounds
____	19. red fern	S.	grew on a sacred spot
____	20. Talequah	T.	location of kennel

ANSWER KEY MATCHING QUIZ 1 *Where the Red Fern Grows*

L	1.	bet	A.	mountain setting of novel
G	2.	bobcat	B.	was amazed by Billy's dogs
O	3.	Cherokee	C.	Grandpa entered the hounds in one
C	4.	contest	D.	last name of Rubin and Rainie
E	5.	fifty	E.	dollar amount Billy saved
R	6.	forty	F.	Billy carried the puppies in one
I	7.	ghost coon	G.	Billy thought he heard one while hunting
M	8.	God	H.	prayed for a way to move to town
P	9.	Grandpa	I.	Billy didn't want to kill it
F	10.	gunny sack	J.	town where Billy picked up his puppies
B	11.	judge	K.	the scourge of the mountains
T	12.	Kentucky	L.	Grandpa made one with Pritchard boys
H	13.	Mama	M.	thought about and talked to frequently by Billy
K	14.	mountain lion	N.	Pritchards' hound
Q	15.	New England	O.	Mama's Indian heritage
N	16.	Old Blue	P.	Billy's strongest supporter
A	17.	Ozarks	Q.	location of coonskin coat fad
D	18.	Pritchard	R.	dollar amount Billy spent on the hounds
S	19.	red fern	S.	grew on a sacred spot
J	20.	Talequah	T.	location of kennel

MATCHING QUIZ 2 Where *the Red Fern Grows*

_____ 1. Billy
_____ 2. cap
_____ 3. coats
_____ 4. depot
_____ 5. flowers
_____ 6. gate post
_____ 7. gold
_____ 8. gun
_____ 9. Illinois
_____ 10. K.C. Baking Powder
_____ 11. Little Ann
_____ 12. marshal
_____ 13. Mr. Ringtail
_____ 14. Old Dan
_____ 15. Oklahoma
_____ 16. Papa
_____ 17. Rainie
_____ 18. reflection
_____ 19. treed
_____ 20. whoop

A. Billy had to wait until he was 21 for one of these
B. fad for these drove the price of skins up
C. Mama made one from Billy's first coonskin
D. saved for two years to buy hound dogs
E. died to be with partner
F. got caught in a muskrat den
G. saved all of Billy's money
H. what the hounds did to the raccoons
I. where the ghost coon hid
J. building where Billy picked up his dogs
K. gave Billy his first taste of soda pop
L. sound Billy made to his dogs
M. Billy first saw his in a window in Talequah
N. Billy's can bank
O. Billy put them on Rubin's grave
P. surviving Pritchard boy
Q. type of cup Billy gave to his youngest sister
R. nickname Billy gave to most coons
S. state where Billy lived
T. river where Billy and dogs hunted

ANSWER KEY MATCHING QUIZ 2 *Where the Red Fern Grows*

D	1.	Billy	A.	Billy had to wait until he was 21 for one of these
C	2.	cap	B.	fad for these drove the price of skins up
B	3.	coats	C.	Mama made one from Billy's first coonskin
J	4.	depot	D.	saved for two years to buy hound dogs
O	5.	flowers	E.	died to be with partner
I	6.	gate post	F.	got caught in a muskrat den
Q	7.	gold	G.	saved all of Billy's money
A	8.	gun	H.	what the hounds did to the raccoons
T	9.	Illinois	I.	where the ghost coon hid
N	10.	K.C. Baking Powder	J.	building where Billy picked up his dogs
E	11.	Little Ann	K.	gave Billy his first taste of soda pop
K	12.	marshal	L.	sound Billy made to his dogs
R	13.	Mr. Ringtail	M.	Billy first saw his in a window in Talequah
F	14.	Old Dan	N.	Billy's can bank
S	15.	Oklahoma	O.	Billy put them on Rubin's grave
G	16.	Papa	P.	surviving Pritchard boy
P	17.	Rainie	Q.	type of cup Billy gave to his youngest sister
M	18.	reflection	R.	nickname Billy gave to most coons
H	19.	treed	S.	state where Billy lived
L	20.	whoop	T.	river where Billy and dogs hunted

JUGGLE LETTER REVIEW GAME *Where the Red Fern Grows*

TBE	BET	Grandpa made one with the Pritchard boys
LILYB	BILLY	was afflicted with "puppy love"
CBOATB	BOBCAT	Billy thought the hounds had treed one
OSTOMTB	BOTTOMS	location of the big sycamore tree
PCA	CAP	Mama made one from Billy's first coon skin
REHEOKEC	CHEROKEE	Mama's Indian heritage
ATSOC	COATS	fad for coon skin ones raised the price of skins
SCOTETN	CONTEST	Grandpa entered the hounds in one
ODPTE	DEPOT	where Billy picked up his puppies
ITFYF	FIFTY	dollar amount Billy saved
LEFRSOW	FLOWERS	Billy put them on Rubin's grave
YOTRF	FORTY	dollar cost of the hounds
AGVTPSTV	GATE POST	where the ghost coon hid
OHSGCOTNO	GHOST COON	Billy didn't want to kill it
DGO	GOD	thought about and talked to frequently by Billy
LOGD	GOLD	cup Billy gave to his youngest sister
ARDANGP	GRANDPA	Billy's strongest supporter
GNU	GUN	Billy's other desire
KUSNGNYAC	GUNNY SACK	Billy carried the puppies home in one
ILINLISO	ILLINOIS	river near the bottoms
UGJED	JUDGE	was amazed at Billy's dogs
UETCKKYN	KENTUCKY	location of kennel
TTANNLILE	LITTLE ANN	smart but gun-shy
AMAM	MAMA	prayed for a way to move to town
ALRMSHA	MARSHAL	rescued Billy from the fight with town children
TMUINLIOAONN	MOUNTAIN LION	attacked Billy and the dogs
RLRITNMGIA	MR. RINGTAIL	nickname for a raccoon
GEWAEDNNLN	NEW ENGLAND	where the coonskin coat fad was
LODAND	OLD DAN	strong and aggressive
LBUOLED	OLD BLUE	the Pritchard's hound
KOMAHOAL	OKLAHOMA	state where Billy lived
RAZOKS	OZARKS	mountain setting of novel
APAP	PAPA	gave Billy three steel traps
RRITHPADC	PRITCHARD	Rubin and Rainie's last name
NAIIRE	RAINIE	was excited on the hunt for the ghost coon
DRERNEF	RED FERN	grew on a sacred spot
EFCRTIOLNE	REFLECTION	Billy saw his for the first time on his trip to town
BRUIN	RUBIN	fell on the axe and died
MIESA	SAMIE	curious cat

ILRVES	SILVER	cup Little Ann won at the beauty contest
LTEES	SLEET	weather during last night of coon hunting contest
ROTES	STORE	where Grandpa worked
LQAUTAHE	TALEQUAH	town Billy walked to for the dogs
NET	TEN	dollar amount Billy spent on gifts for the family
EHRET	THREE	number of Billy's sisters
EREDT	TREED	what the hounds did to the coons
TOW	TWO	dollar amount of Grandpa's bet with Pritchards
POWOH	WHOOP	sound Billy made to the hounds
WIRLONSALSW	WILSON RAWLS	author

VOCABULARY RESOURCE MATERIALS

VOCABULARY WORD SEARCH *Where the Red Fern Grows*

All the words in this list are associated with *Where the Red Fern Grows* with emphasis on the vocabulary words being studied in the unit. The words are placed backwards, forward, diagonally up and down. The clues below the word search will help identify the word.

```
J P C B C P T E N D D Q P F U D I G H K R R C V C H G L L Y R U N X
K Z A E Y O H J H J U E O A Y Q O K N S C D N O O G O H I L E J T L
M C R G P T N M I T O A K M Z P H M Z I J T A P M Y X C M T B K P N
W S E R N R I V H F G P F N F K S S A B Y X P T M D U O B N O I J Q
B O S U T I E R E D E L Q A Y U R G X I Q A U Y O Z R L E A S Q T G
C O S D A J R D A N K N I L X U H N Y Z N R B P T D G H R L O C U A
N Q N G E X N E A I I K L H B D X X F N E N H D I X L T W A T Y Q S
S K Q I F R O S P T L E K Q Q Z U L C C I H K G O N Y V K H I Z A A
I W Q N A S I M E M O U N A I C I C T X R J L E N O J E I C J S X Q
A D N G T W T S J X A R C T G V T C T K E A C S M T B F Y N A F C G
L C M L Q H O J V S T H Y E E I D K E L E E T R D S Y S N O H C K R
J V C Y W X N T F D B W I L P D N M S V R B R N I H M T T N Z L Q D
A K Q M U L L E D R O O L Y C E N X W R P J B B A X Y A D A H A Q Q
W W S S Q W W I L E Y I Y U Y X W R B Z Y D L L Y I A E Q E C Y B R
A S T O N I S H E D G W T Q F Z V E R G E H H C O C F G O L Z L A Q
G W I Y G X U C U E H N I R W C X N S S H V P L C Y K E Z C D A E S
N L I U Q H Y N R P U O F G H D Y A Y C D Q M B P B E K D O G P D H
D Q O B U Q D E W X D F B H P M Y A G R O E N T K C E X R P A C E K
P W L A J S N U M L U N G E P L C G W K S E M T V M N M Q I M M P V
H U F D T T Q Q D F Y V P W B F L K W H Z G V K Z O A K U M Z L L L
G W I T P E U D X U U K M F Z W X U N C O Z L P Y N V I C I O U S O
O R Z R Y J D B S S K T J E F I J B L R W S N W T L E Z L Q F T J Y
```

ASTONISHED	DORMANT	NOTION
BAYING	EERIE	OBSTACLE
BEGRUDGINGLY	GLOATED	PACE
BELLIGERENT	HAMPERING	PECULIARITY
CARESS	KEEN	PREDATORY
COMMOTION	LIMBER	QUENCH
CONVENIENT	LULL	SOBER
DAZED	LUNGE	VERGE
DEFIANT	MULLED	VICIOUS
DOMAIN	NONCHALANTLY	WILEY

VOCABULARY CROSSWORD *Where the Red Fern Grows*

VOCABULARY CROSSWORD CLUES *Where the Red Fern Grows*

ACROSS
1 Destructively or frenetically violent
3 Gone over extensively in the mind
6 Walk with short steps that tilt the body from side to side
9 Having a fine, sharp cutting edge or point
10 A gentle touch or gesture of fondness, tenderness, or love
11 Removed or forced out from a position of dwelling
13 Cunning
16 Bending or flexing readily; pliable
19 Marked by an aggressive disposition; savage
20 Railroad or bus station
23 The point beyond which an action is likely to begin
24 Cause to be sorrowful; distress
26 Deep ditch or channel cut in the earth by running water
28 Depression or hollow, usually filled with deep mud or mire
29 Latent but capable of being activated; sleeping
31 Hanging loosely or swinging
32 Unconcerned or indifferently
33 Satisfy

DOWN
1 Crying or sobbing loudly; wailing
2 Serious, grave, or solemn
3 Protruding shelf over a fireplace
4 A relatively calm interval
5 Projecting overhang at the lower edge of a roof
7 Put out; extinguished
8 The rate of speed at which something is done
11 Severe or radical in nature; extreme
12 Stunned
13 Deep distress or misery, as from grief; wretchedness
14 Strange and frightening
15 Shook with a slight, rapid, tremulous movement
16 Marked by effortless grace
17 Inclined to fight; hostile or aggressive
18 Sudden forward movement or plunge
21 Living by hunting
22 With great care or delicacy; cautiously
24 Expressed great, often malicious, pleasure or self-satisfaction
25 Pierced or penetrated
27 Uttering a deep, prolonged bark
28 Widespread, dreadful affliction and devastation
29 Territory over which rule or control is exercised
30 Mental image; idea or conception

VOCABULARY CROSSWORD ANSWER KEY *Where the Red Fern Grows*

B	E	R	S	E	R	K			S						M	U	L	L	E	D	
A									O						A		U		A		
W	A	D	D	L	E		P		B			K	E	E	N		L		V		
L		O				C	A	R	E	S	S				T		L		E		
		U					C		R						E				S		
D	I	S	L	O	D	G	E	D					W	I	L	E	Y				
R		E			A								O			E		Q			
A		D			Z				L	I	M	B	E	R		R		U		L	
S					E				I			E			V	I	C	I	O	U	S
T					D	E	P	O	T			L				E		V		N	
I				G			R		H			L					V	E	R	G	E
C		G	R	I	E	V	E		E			I		C				R		E	
		L		N			D					G	U	L	L	Y		E			B
S	L	O	U	G	H		A					E		E				D			A
C		A		E			T			D	O	R	M	A	N	T			N		Y
O		T		R			O			O		E		V					O		I
U		E		L			R			M		N		E					T		N
R		D		Y			Y			A		T		D	A	N	G	L	I	N	G
G										I									O		
E		N	O	N	C	H	A	L	A	N	Y	L	Y			Q	U	E	N	C	H

VOCABULARY WORKSHEET 1 *Where the Red Fern Grows*

____	1. astonished	A.	living by hunting other organisms
____	2. begrudgingly	B.	strange and frightening
____	3. belligerent	C.	pierced or penetrated
____	4. cleaved	D.	explored; investigated
____	5. commotion	E.	an agitated disturbance
____	6. dazed	F.	filled with astonishment or perplexity
____	7. depot	G.	reluctantly
____	8. domain	H.	marked by effortless grace
____	9. doused	I.	a railroad or bus station
____	10. dumbfounded	J.	serious, grave, or solemn
____	11. eerie	K.	gone over extensively in the mind; pondered
____	12. hampering	L.	filled with sudden wonder or amazement
____	13. lithe	M.	a territory over which rule or control is exercised
____	14. mulled	N.	rate of speed at which a person walks or runs
____	15. notion	O.	inclined or eager to fight; hostile
____	16. pace	P.	put out; extinguished
____	17. predatory	Q.	a mental image or idea
____	18. probed	R.	stunned, stupefied
____	19. scourge	S.	widespread affliction and devastation
____	20. sober	T.	preventing free movement or progress

ANSWER KEY VOCABULARY WORKSHEET 1 *Where the Red Fern Grows*

L	1.	astonished	A.	living by hunting other organisms
G	2.	begrudgingly	B.	strange and frightening
O	3.	belligerent	C.	pierced or penetrated
C	4.	cleaved	D.	explored; investigated
E	5.	commotion	E.	an agitated disturbance
R	6.	dazed	F.	filled with astonishment or perplexity
I	7.	depot	G.	reluctantly
M	8.	domain	H.	marked by effortless grace
P	9.	doused	I.	a railroad or bus station
F	10.	dumbfounded	J.	serious, grave, or solemn
B	11.	eerie	K.	gone over extensively in the mind; pondered
T	12.	hampering	L.	filled with sudden wonder or amazement
H	13.	lithe	M.	a territory over which rule or control is exercised
K	14.	mulled	N.	rate of speed at which a person walks or runs
Q	15.	notion	O.	inclined or eager to fight; hostile
N	16.	pace	P.	put out; extinguished
A	17.	predatory	Q.	a mental image or idea
D	18.	probed	R.	stunned, stupefied
S	19.	scourge	S.	widespread affliction and devastation
J	20.	sober	T.	preventing free movement or progress

VOCABULARY WORKSHEET 2 *Where the Red Fern Grows*

____ 1. **boldly resisting**
A. bustling B. hampering C. dazed D. defiant

____ 2. **latent but capable of being activated**
A. berserk B. predatory C. dormant D. wiley

____ 3. **the projecting overhang at the lower edge of a roof**
A. gully B. eaves C. slough D. mantel

____ 4. **expressed malicious self satisfaction**
A. cleaved B. gloated C. quenched D. mulled

____ 5. **having a sharp, fine cutting edge or point**
A. keen B. eerie C. convenient D. wiley

____ 6. **a relatively calm interval**
A. caress B. scourge C. notion D. lull

____ 7. **a sudden forward movement**
A. bawl B. lunge C. commotion D. obstacle

____ 8. **unconcernedly or indifferently**
A. squalling B. peculiarity C. nonchalantly D. dangling

____ 9. **made a V-shaped cut in**
A. notched B. cleaved C. quivered D. probed

____ 10. **gently rubbing or pushing against**
A. hampering B. dangling C. nuzzling D. gnawing

____ 11. **sudden sharp spasms of pain**
A. pangs B. pace C. grieve D. caress

____ 12. **unpleasant or troublesome situation**
A. commotion B. squabble C. notion D. predicament

____ 13. **to satisfy**
A. slough B. quench C. verge D. coaxing

____ 14. **shook with a slight, rapid movement**
A. grieve B. probed C. dislodged D. quivered

____ 15. **a depression or hollow, usually filled with mud**
A. slough B. caress C. gully D. verge

____ 16. **a noisy quarrel**
A. squalling B. convenient C. squabble D. domain

____ 17. **the point beyond which an action is likely to begin**
A. dangling B. mantel C. obstacle D. verge

____ 18. **having an aggressive disposition**
A. wiley B. vicious C. sober D. lithe

____ 19. **to walk with short steps that tilt the body from side to side**
A. bawl B. dormant C. waddle D. doused

____ 20. **deep distress or misery**
A. woe B. scourge C. slough D. notion

ANSWER KEY VOCABULARY WORKSHEET 2 *Where the Red Fern Grows*

D   1.   **boldly resisting**
       A. bustling   B. hampering   C. dazed   **D. defiant**

C   2.   **latent but capable of being activated**
       A. berserk   B. predatory   **C. dormant**   D. wiley

B   3.   **the projecting overhang at the lower edge of a roof**
       A. gully   **B. eaves**   C. slough   D. mantel

B   4.   **expressed malicious self satisfaction**
       A. cleaved   **B. gloated**   C. quenched   D. mulled

A   5.   **having a sharp, fine cutting edge or point**
       A. keen   B. eerie   C. convenient   D. wiley

D   6.   **a relatively calm interval**
       A. caress   B. scourge   C. notion   **D. lull**

B   7.   **a sudden forward movement**
       A. bawl   **B. lunge**   C. commotion   D. obstacle

C   8.   **unconcernedly or indifferently**
       A. squalling   B. peculiarity   **C. nonchalantly**   D. dangling

A   9.   **made a V-shaped cut in**
       A. notched   B. cleaved   C. quivered   D. probed

C   10.   **gently rubbing or pushing against**
       A. hampering   B. dangling   **C. nuzzling**   D. gnawing

A   11.   **sudden sharp spasms of pain**
       A. pangs   B. pace   C. grieve   D. caress

D   12.   **unpleasant or troublesome situation**
       A. commotion   B. squabble   C. notion   **D. predicament**

B   13.   **to satisfy**
       A. slough   **B. quench**   C. verge   D. coaxing

D   14.   **shook with a slight, rapid movement**
       A. grieve   B. probed   C. dislodged   **D. quivered**

A   15.   **a depression or hollow, usually filled with mud**
       A. slough   B. caress   C. depot   D. verge

C   16.   **a noisy quarrel**
       A. squalling   B. convenient   **C. squabble**   D. domain

D   17.   **the point beyond which an action is likely to begin**
       A. dangling   B. mantel   C. obstacle   **D. verge**

B   18.   **having an aggressive disposition**
       A. wiley   **B. vicious**   C. sober   D. lithe

C   19.   **to walk with short steps that tilt the body from side to side**
       A. bawl   B. dormant   **C. waddle**   D. doused

A   20.   **deep distress or misery**
       A. woe   B. scourge   C. slough   D. notion

JUGGLE LETTER VOCABULARY REVIEW GAME *Where the Red Fern Grows*

SCRAMBLED	WORDS	CLUES
HNASISEODT	ASTONISHED	filled with sudden wonder or amazement
WALB	BAWL	crying or sobbing loudly; wailing
NYIBGA	BAYING	uttering a deep, prolonged bark
RUYEGDIBNGLG	BEGRUDGINGLY	reluctantly
NBEIELGETLR	BELLIGERENT	inclined or eager to fight; hostile or aggressive
RESRBKE	BERSERK	destructively or frenetically violent
SBGTUINV	BUSTLING	moving energetically and busily
SAECSR	CARESS	a gentle touch or gesture of fondness, tenderness, or love
DELVCEA	CLEAVED	pierced or penetrated
XAINCOG	COAXING	persuading or trying to persuade by pleading or flattery
TOMOICONM	COMMOTION	an agitated disturbance
NECNOVIETN	CONVENIENT	easy to reach; accessible
NGDNAIGL	DANGLING	hanging loosely or swinging
EZADD	DAZED	stunned, stupefied
EDANFTI	DEFIANT	boldly resisting
POETD	DEPOT	a railroad or bus station
DODGILEDS	DISLODGED	removed or forced out from a position or dwelling
MOANID	DOMAIN	a territory over which rule or control is exercised
MORANDT	DORMANT	latent but capable of being activated
OSDEUD	DOUSED	put out; extinguished
RATDICS	DRASTIC	severe or radical in nature; extreme
UODBFUNDEDM	DUMBFOUNDED	filled with astonishment and perplexity
VASEE	EAVES	the projecting overhang at the lower edge of a roof
IREEE	EERIE	strange and frightening
ERNILGYG	GINGERLY	with great care or delicacy; cautiously
LODATEG	GLOATED	expressed great, often malicious, pleasure or self-satisfaction
WAGINGN	GNAWING	afflicting or worrying persistently
IGERVE	GRIEVE	to cause to be sorrowful; distress
LULYG	GULLY	a deep ditch or channel cut in the earth by running water
MGAERINPH	HAMPERING	preventing the free movement, action, or progress of
EKEN	KEEN	having a fine, sharp cutting edge or point
BRIMEL	LIMBER	bending or flexing readily; pliable.
HETLI	LITHE	marked by effortless grace

JUGGLE LETTER CLUE SHEET *Where the Red Fern Grows*

SCRAMBLED	WORDS	CLUES
LLUL	LULL	a relatively calm interval
NGLUE	LUNGE	a sudden forward movement or plunge
ANELTM	MANTEL	the protruding shelf over a fireplace
ULMELD	MULLED	gone over extensively in the mind
HONCNALYANTL	NONCHALANTLY	unconcernedly or indifferently
TOCNEDH	NOTCHED	made a V-shaped cut
NOOTNI	NOTION	a mental image or representation; an idea or conception
ZUNZLIGN	NUZZLING	gently rubbing or pushing against
LABSTOCE	OBSTACLE	one that opposes, stands in the way of, or holds up progress
CAEP	PACE	the rate of speed at which a person walks or runs
AGPSN	PANGS	sudden sharp spasms of pain
TAPEULIRIYC	PECULIARITY	a notable or distinctive feature or characteristic
TDRREAOYP	PREDATORY	living by hunting other organisms
DREIMCAENTP	PREDICAMENT	an unpleasant or troublesome situation that is hard to get out of
BEDROP	PROBED	explored; investigated
CQENHU	QUENCH	to satisfy
VRUIEQED	QUIVERED	shook with a slight, rapid, tremulous movement
GCORUES	SCOURGE	widespread, dreadful affliction and devastation
LOSGHU	SLOUGH	a depression or hollow, usually filled with deep mud or mire
BEORS	SOBER	serious, grave, or solemn
BSQLUABE	SQUABBLE	a noisy quarrel, usually about a trivial matter
NQLALSUIG	SQUALLING	screaming or crying loudly and harshly
GEREV	VERGE	the point beyond which an action, is likely to begin; the brink
IVIOSCU	VICIOUS	marked by an aggressive disposition; savage.
DADEWL	WADDLE	to walk with short steps that tilt the body from side to side.
LEWYI	WILEY	cunning.
OWE	WOE	deep distress or misery, as from grief; wretchedness

www.ingramcontent.com/pod-product-compliance
Lightning Source LLC
Chambersburg PA
CBHW051410070526
44584CB00023B/3363